2's Art EXPERIENCE

Crayons
Doughs
Paints
Chalks
Papers
& MORE !

2's Art EXPERIENCE

by
Liz & Dick Wilmes

Illustrations by
Janet McDonnell

A  Publication

38W567 Brindlewood, Elgin, Illinois   60123

ART

Cover Design and Graphics: David VanDelinder
STUDIO 155
Elgin, Illinois

Computer Graphics: Jeane Heckert
VISION MAKER GRAPHICS
Elgin, Illinois

Text Graphics: Janet McDonnell
Early Childhood Illustrator
Arlington Heights, Illinois

SPECIAL THANKS TO:
Cheryl Luppino and Mary Schuring for sharing so many ideas, activities, and special hints, so we can all help young children, get even more involved in their dramatic play.

PUBLISHED BY:

38W567 Brindlewood
Elgin, Illinois 60123

ISBN 0-943452-21-X

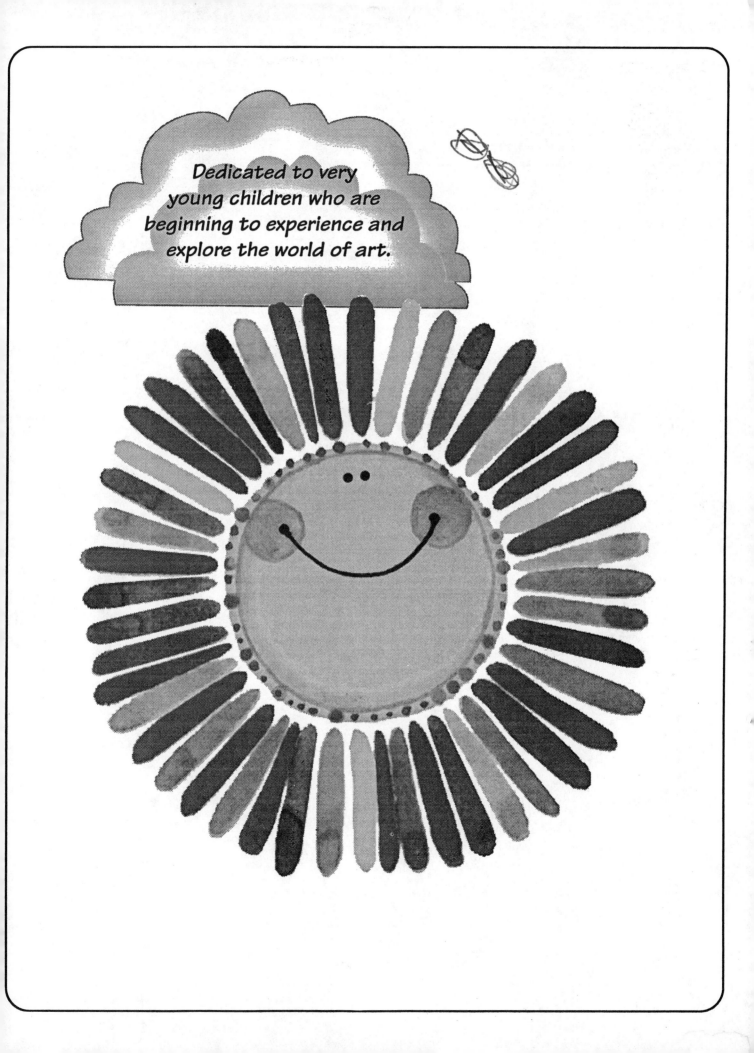

Dedicated to very young children who are beginning to experience and explore the world of art.

CONTENTS

INTRODUCTION

USING CRAYONS, PENCILS, AND MARKERS

USING DOUGHS

USING PAINTS

USING FINGERPAINTS

USING GLUES AND PASTES

USING CHALKS

USING EASELS

APPENDICES
ART CHARTS

Art With Toddlers and Two's

1. Respect children's art

☛ Let children use the art materials for as long as they would like.

☛ Set up the same art activity several days in a row. Maybe change it slightly.

  ~ New prop
  ~ Different color
  ~ Variety of paper

☛ Encourage the children to use materials and supplies over and over again ~~ they enjoy the process. They like to:

  ~ Scribble with crayons, pencils, etc.
  ~ Smear with sponges and other printing props.
  ~ Drizzle glue out of squeeze bottles.
  ~ Pound, poke, and squeeze dough.
  ~ Feel the *"sticky quality"* of paste and glue.

☛ If you are writing children's names on the art, let the children tell you where they want their names.

☛ Let children take their art home or appropriately display it in the classroom.

☛ Talk with children about their art.

☛ Ask children if they would like to *"Do it again?"*

2. Make clean-up easier

☛ Have children wear smocks.

☛ Use easy-to-wash containers.

☛ Do very messy art activities in large containers such as: the sand/water table, messy trays, bussing tubs, or dish tubs.

☛ Let the children help clean-up.

☛ Keep mops, sponges, and paper towels handy.

3. Help children control their art

☛ Use an ART TARP - a large painter's cotton drop cloth:

The ART TARP helps keep the floor and table clean, and defines the space where the art activity is occurring. Use it especially when the children are painting, but it's great for any messy art.

~ Put the TARP on the floor. Set your activity on it.
~ Put the TARP on your art table. Let the children work right on it.
~ Let the TARP dry. When art is over, fold up the TARP for next time.
~ Wash the TARP as needed.

☛ Use washable, unbreakable trays on the art table.

☛ Tape paper and other surfaces to the table, floor, or ART TARP.

☛ Help children put their art in a safe place, after they have finished.

4. Remember safety

☛ When using an electrical appliance:

~ Tape the cord to the floor.
~ Keep unused plugs covered.
~ Set up activities in quiet places in the room.
~ Keep the appliance away from the edge of the table.

☛ Use materials which children cannot easily put in their mouths.

☛ Mop up spilled water and paint immediately.

☛ Use non-toxic paints and other media.

Using Different Media With Toddlers and Two's

1. When using crayons

☛ When using a <u>few</u> <u>crayons</u>, tie long pieces of string to one end of each crayon, and tape or tie the opposite ends of the strings to the tables, easels, or counter tops that the children are using.

☛ Let the children color with lots of different types of crayons -- chunky, fat, soap, etc.

☛ Offer children crayons with and without the paper wrapping.

2. When using fingerpaint

☛ Children's main motivation is the *"feel"* of the paint.
  ~ Use a variety of surfaces.
  ~ Put textures in the paint.
  ~ Fingerpaint with a variety of *"paints."*

☛ Keep the surface moist so the paint, shaving cream, etc. moves easily. Keep a small spray bottle of water nearby to moisten the surface or the children's fingers.

3. When using glue and paste

☛ Put glue in small squeeze bottles. Refill each bottle as necessary.

☛ Put glue in jar tops and let the children brush glue on the paper, boxes, etc.

☛ Use home-made glue as often as possible -- it is much less expensive and is great for drizzling.

4. When using dough

☛ Put out doughs which are soft and easy to squeeze, poke, pound, squish, etc.

☛ Make sure the dough is room temperature -- cold dough is difficult to manipulate.

☛ Add props for variation -- small wooden mallets, large jar lids, etc.

☛ Let the children help you make no-cook doughs.

5. When using paint

☛ Put the ART TARP on the table or floor.

☛ Add a little liquid dish soap to the tempera paint.

☛ Pour minimal amounts of paint in the containers. Add more paint as necessary.

☛ When painting with props, attach handles to objects which are difficult to hold. For example:

   ~ Hot glue (or white glue) knobs on container lids, sponges, puzzle pieces, etc.
   ~ Insert popsicle sticks into ice cubes.

☛ When painting with brushes, use ones with short, blunt handles.

6. When using chalk

☛ Use lots of different surfaces.

☛ Erasing is just as important and fun as chalking.

Involve Your Families

Familiarize the families in your program with the art activities you plan for the children. Through this ongoing involvement, parents will:

- ☛ Learn more about their children's development.

- ☛ Gain insight into your classroom.

- ☛ Develop an appreciation for the skills their children are learning.

- ☛ Encourage their children to be involved with all of the art activities you offer.

- ☛ Talk with their children about the art they bring home.

Involve Your Families Through

Your Newsletter

In the regular newsletter you distribute to your families, highlight different art activities the children have experienced. Think about adding a photograph showing the children doing an activity. Remember, *"A picture is worth a thousand words."*

Volunteering

Ask volunteers to help children in the art area. Before they join the children, tell the volunteers about the activity the children are doing, and give them some hints about talking with the children concerning their art.

Volunteers can also help the children frame and hang the artwork that is going to be displayed.

Explanation Cards

In the corner of each art activity being displayed, add a short descriptive note which explains the art media the children used and how they used it. Encourage the parents to read the notes and talk with their children about the experience.

Painters used feather dusters and scrub brushes.

Art Festival

In conjunction with a regular parent meeting, display a wide variety of art the children have recently been enjoying. As a part of the meeting, explain the different types of art. You might include a short slide presentation showing the children in the art area.

Donate Materials

At the beginning of the year give your parents a list of art materials you'll be using during the year. (See next page for a sample list -- Want Ads.) Encourage parents to save these items and donate them to the school. Throughout the year they will enjoy seeing the materials, as their children use them for individual and group art activities.

Want Ads

DISPOSABLE SUPPLIES

Cardboard soda carriers
Crayons
Fabric
Large piece styrofoam
Paper
  Boxes
  Cardboard
  Cardboard tubes
  Grocery bags
  Paper plates
  Textured paper
  Wallpaper
  Wrapping paper
Plastic milk bottles
Ribbon
Rubber bands
Shoe boxes
Sponges
String
Twine
Yarn

PRINTING PROPS

Berry baskets
Biscuit cutters
Cookie cutters
Funnels
Thick sponges
Spools
Wide jar lids

BUILDING BLOCKS

Elgin, Illinois 60123

PERMANENT SUPPLIES

Bricks
Bubble pack
Castors
Chalkboards
Clothesline
Clothespins
Door mats
Formica
Ice cube trays
Measuring cups
Mittens
Mixing bowls
Muffin tins

Pails
Paint brushes
Paint rollers
Pegboard
Plastic carpet protectors
Plastic place mats
Plastic trays
Popsicle molds
Pump-type bottles
Record player
Rubber bath mats
Scoops
Stools
Warming tray

CONTAINERS

Brownie pans
Coffee cans
Dish tubs
Margarine tubs
Meat/produce trays

Pie pans
Pitchers
Squeeze bottles
Unbreakable shaker
   bottles

FAMILIES

If you have any of these items at home, please send them to school with your child.

THANKS

Elgin, Illinois 60123

Displaying Children's Art

**Show appreciation and respect for children's art.
When displaying it, remember to:**

☛ Hang the children's individual and group art at their eye level, so they can easily see it.

☛ Hang the art straight. Use the lines in the walls, frames in the window, borders on the bulletin boards, and grain in the doors as reference points.

☛ Check each morning to be certain that all the artwork is securely fastened. Re-hang any that might have come loose or have fallen off.

☛ Use heavy-duty tape when the surface is difficult to display on. Loop the tape in circles, attach it to the back of the art, and then fasten it to the wall or door. Doing it this way, the tape does not interfere with the art. If the surface is easy to hang on, doublestick cellophane tape works well.

☛ Talk with the children about their art. Encourage their comments and reactions. Discuss color, the medium and props they used, how they did the art, who they did the art with, and so on.

> ~ *"You covered your paper with red paint!"*
> ~ *"You and Jamie are poking so many holes in the dough."*
> ~ *"Isabel, you are fingerpainting with red and yellow paint."*

Framing Children's Art

Framing children's art helps to show it off. It sends a special message to the children that you respect their work and feel it is important. You or a volunteer can easily frame art with children.

PLACEMAT FRAMES

Encourage your parents to donate clean cloth/plastic placemats which they no long need. Use them in several different ways:

☛ Put a long, low table in your hallway or entrance. Tape or pin the children's art to the mats. Lay the framed art on the table. Encourage parents and other visitors to look at the art. Change it often, so adults and children are always encouraged to see, *"What's new!"*

☛ Staple/sew the mats in a patchwork design. Attach them to a bulletin board. When a child finishes an art activity, let him choose a placemat to frame his work, and then help him tape it on.

☛ Sew several placemats into a long strip for your door. Attach artwork to it.

PAPER PLATE FRAMES

Hang pieces of children's art in various small areas of the room, such as on a wall next to the cubbies, in the bathroom, just outside the door, under the windows, etc.

To make the frames you'll need: paper plates, pizza boards, and self-adhesive Velcro ® dots. Put one side of each Velcro ® dot on the wall where you want to hang art. Put the opposite sides of the dots on the backs of the plates/boards. Stick the plates/boards on the wall. Now the frames are ready.

When a child wants to hang his art on one of these frames, put a circle of tape on the back of the art, and stick it to the plate/board.

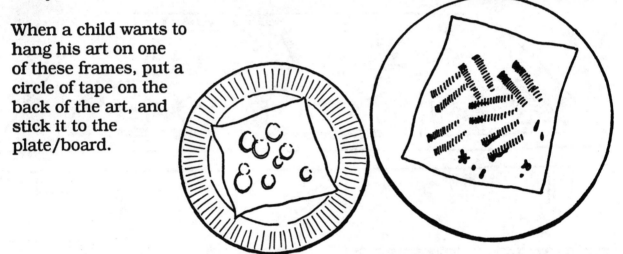

FABRIC AND WRAPPING PAPER FRAMES

Glue children's larger creations to pieces of fabric or wrapping paper. This really helps them come alive!

Water down white glue, brush it on the back of the artwork, and then press the art to the background. Trim the edges of the frame with regular scissors or pinking shears.

PAPER SACK FRAMES

Use large paper sacks like those from the grocery store, and display several pieces of art together in the same frame.

☛ Cut openings in the bags a little smaller than the artwork you're going to frame. Brush glue around the front edges of the art, carefully slide it into the bag, and line it up with the opening you cut. Press the art so it adheres to the inside of the bag.

You can use all sides of the bag and hang it from the ceiling, or use three sides and display it on a wall or bulletin board.

☛ Let each child brush watered-down glue on the back of his art, and then put it on an empty space on a bag. Rub the art gently so it sticks well. Next, dip a heavy piece of yarn into the watered-down glue, pull it out, rub the excess glue off the yarn, and then put it around the art.

When the bag is full of art, hang it from your ceiling.

Constructing Simple Displays

COLORFUL CATERPILLAR
Great way to display lots of art!

Use the pattern on the next page and make a large caterpillar face. Using a circle of heavy-duty tape, attach the face to your wall. Cut out lots of large wallpaper or construction paper circles for the body. Keep them handy.

When a child finishes a piece of art, ask him if he'd like to hang it on the caterpillar. If he wants, give him a wallpaper/construction paper circle, and help him tape his art to it. Then attach the art to the end of the caterpillar.

When a child wants to take his art home, simply remove the art from the circle and give it to the child. Leave the circle on the wall, and let that child or another child display another piece of art on it.

Let your caterpillar grow with all of the children's art. He may soon wiggle along the entire wall.

COLORFUL CATERPILLAR

CURLY QUES

Use a *"curly que"* to display small pieces of art that the children create.

Get a piece of heavy posterboard. Draw a spiral on it as large as you can, and then cut it out. Punch holes along the spiral, and tie a piece of yarn/ribbon through each one. Punch a hole at the top, tie a long piece of heavy twine through it, and hang the *"curly que"* from the ceiling.

When each child is ready to hang his artwork, attach his art to one of the pieces of yarn or ribbon.

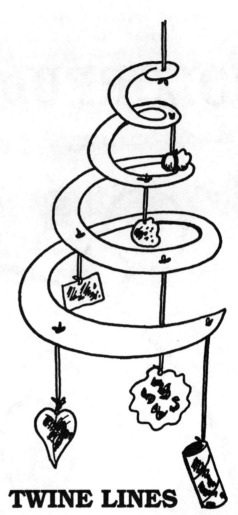

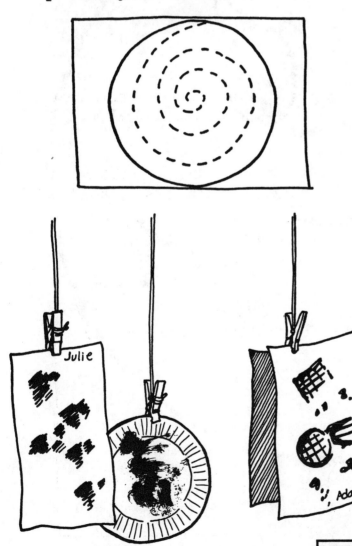

TWINE LINES

"Twine lines" are very easy, attractive, and versatile displays.

You'll need a ball of heavy twine and spring-loaded clothespins. Hang varying lengths of twine from your ceiling so you can easily reach them. Tie a clothespin to the end of each piece.

When the children finish their art, let them choose which piece of twine they would like to display it on. Clip it on.

HINT: Remember, you can display two pieces of art from the same clothespin by hanging them back-to-back.

COLORFUL HANGERS

Add pizazz and color to your room by stringing a piece of colorful garland or wide ribbon across an area.

Hang it securely and a little taut, because as you add art, it will begin to sag to an appropriate level. Use colored, plastic clothespins to attach the art.

HANGER BANNERS

"Hanger banners" are easy to make and very versatile, since they hang in any part of the room where there are hooks. You can also easily tape them to walls and doors, because the hooks in the hangers are flat and lay against any surface.

To make the banner you'll need a roll of shelf paper. Cut a strip as long as you want. Fold the corners of one end over the top of the hanger, and glue the flaps to the backside of the strip.

Let the children clip their art to the banner.

VARIATION: Instead of using shelf paper, use strips of heavy-duty fabric, such as denim, burlap, or canvas.

CRISS-CROSS MOBILE

"Criss-cross mobiles" can easily be left up year 'round. Use them to easily rotate the children's art.

To make each mobile, cross two branches and securely fasten them in the middle with heavy twine. Attach a long piece of twine to the middle for the hanger. Cut varying lengths of heavy-duty yarn and tie them to the branches. Tie a clothespin to the end of each piece of yarn.

When children finish their art, clip it to the mobile.

FISH NET HANGER

If you have a large, empty wall, get a fish net or old hammock and fasten it to the wall. Hang the children's art on it with clothespins.

EXTENSION: During different seasons and holidays add specific decorations to reflect a certain spirit.

- ☛ Weave crepe paper, color ribbons, streamers, or garlands in and out of the holes.

- ☛ Hang small lights around the edges of the netting. (SAFETY: Be sure the netting is fire-proof.)

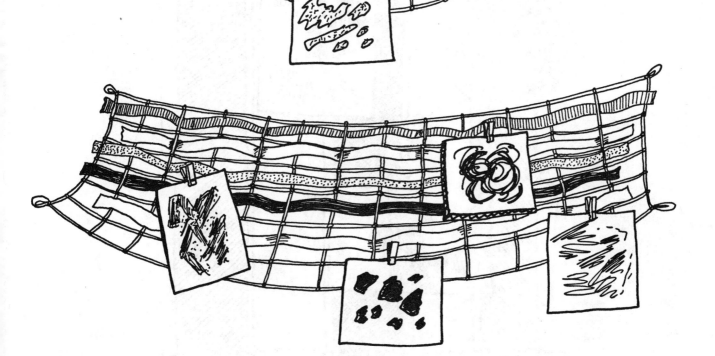

RAINBOW RIBBONS

Make several *"rainbow ribbons"* and hang them in different areas of your room. They add lots of color and cheer, and serve as a display and small divider at the same time.

FOR EACH HANGER, YOU'LL NEED:
- ~ two half-inch dowel rods
- ~ at least five different colors of about 4" wide sturdy ribbon or fabric.

MAKE:
- ~ Cut the ribbons into four foot lengths.
- ~ Wrap one end of each ribbon around one of the dowel rods.
- ~ Securely glue the ribbon to the rod.
- ~ Repeat with the other dowel rod. (Instead of gluing the ribbon/ fabric to the rods, you could sew a rod pocket at both ends of each ribbon and slide the rods through the openings.)
- ~ Attach a piece of heavy-duty twine to each end of one dowel rod, and hang the banner from your ceiling.

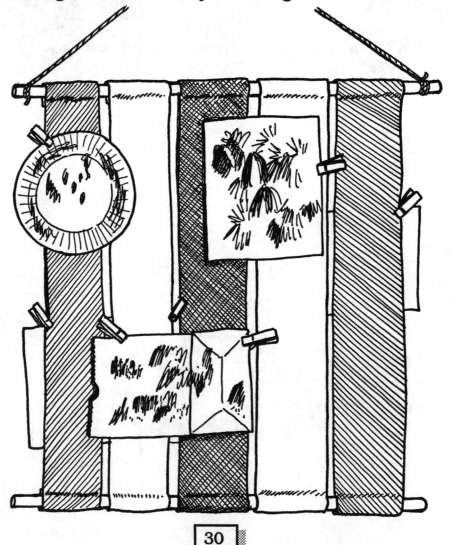

EASY CEILING HANGING

This *"ceiling hanging"* makes it easy to hang murals children have done. You may want to make several. They are great displays.

MAKE:
- ~ Cut 4, 3-foot pieces of twine.
- ~ Attach them to your ceiling so they hang in the corners of a 4' x 8' rectangle.
- ~ Tie a clothespin to the end of each piece of twine.

HANG:
- ~ Let the mural dry.
- ~ Clip a clothespin securely to each corner of the mural.

Using Crayons, Markers, and Pencils

EVERYDAY COLORING

SIZE OF GROUP: Small or large group
DO THE ACTIVITY: At Any Table

SUPPLIES AND MATERIALS

Crayons
Any type of large plain paper, such as:
  Newsprint
  Butcher paper
  Mailing paper
  Shelf paper

PREPARATION

☛ Put different colored crayons in several small containers.

☛ Cut the paper to fit on the table you will be using.

ACTIVITY

Tape the large sheet of paper to the table. Have the crayons nearby.

When a child wants to color, give him a crayon or let him choose one from a container. Let him *"scribble"* for as long as he wants. Maybe he will want to change crayons and color some more.

HINTS

☛ Children love this simple activity. In fact it is a great way to begin your day. Have the paper taped to the table when the children arrive. Let them color for as long as each would like.

☛ Coloring is very soothing for toddlers and twos, thus it makes a great activity when the children are becoming disruptive. Simply tape paper to a table and let the children color.

☛ Coloring is a very social activity -- another good reason to begin each day with crayons.

OUTSIDE COLORING

SIZE OF GROUP: Small group
DO THE ACTIVITY: Outside

SUPPLIES AND MATERIALS

Crayons
Butcher paper
Plastic pool

PREPARATION

☞ Cut butcher paper to fit in your plastic pool.

ACTIVITY

Bring the sheets of butcher paper and crayons outside. Put the pool in a shady area, and lay a piece of paper in it. Keep the bag of crayons in your pocket.

When a child wants to color, open the bag of crayons and let him choose one. If necessary, walk with him over to the pool and help him get started. Let him color for as long as he'd like.

When the paper is full of color, clip it to the fence for everyone to see. Put another piece in the pool, and let the coloring continue.

SOAP CRAYON RECIPE

mix ~ mold

SUPPLIES AND MATERIALS

4 cups of soap powder
1/2 cup water
Food coloring (optional)
Muffin tin

MAKE THE CRAYONS

1. Pour the soap powder in a large bowl.

2. Add the food coloring to the water. (optional)

3. Slowly pour the colored water into the soap powder, stirring while pouring. Add more food coloring if the mixture is not bright enough. Keep stirring until all of the ingredients are well mixed.

4. Press the mixture into the muffin tin cups.

5. Let dry overnight and then pop out your soap crayons!

6. Repeat the activity to make different colors of SOAP CRAYONS.

STORE THE SOAP CRAYONS

Keep your crayons in a large covered margarine tub.

SOAP CRAYON FUN

smear ~ scribble

SIZE OF GROUP: Small group
DO THE ACTIVITY: In the Water Table

SUPPLIES AND MATERIALS

Soap crayons (See recipe on page 36)

PREPARATION

None

ACTIVITY

Have the children push up their sleeves. Give the children soap crayons and let them *"smear"* and *scribble"* all over the inside of the water table. After awhile let the children switch crayons and color with different ones.

EXTENSION

CLEAN THE WATER TABLE

The next day have several sponges, a dish pan filled with a little water, and paper towels available. Let the children wash and dry the water table.

Day One   **Day Two**

CRAYON CLUMPS

SIZE OF GROUP: Small or large group
DO THE ACTIVITY: At the Art Table

SUPPLIES AND MATERIALS

Old, short crayons
Masking tape
Black and white pages of the newspaper
Muffin tin

PREPARATION

☛ Make the Crayon Clumps
1. Peel the paper wrapping off the top portion of each crayon.
2. Gather 4-5 crayons together
3. Tightly wrap the bottom half of the clump with masking tape.
4. Repeat the process for each crayon clump.

☛ Set the CRAYON CLUMPS in a muffin tin.

ACTIVITY

Tape large sheets of newspaper to the table.
Give the children CRAYON CLUMPS and
let them *"scribble"* on the paper for as long
as they want. Encourage them to *"twist"*
their clumps around and color with the
different sides.

VARIATION

Instead of making CRAYON
CLUMPS, make PENCIL
PACKS with
colored pencils.

COLOR TO MUSIC

listen ~ color

SIZE OF GROUP: Small or large group
DO THE ACTIVITY: At the Art Table

SUPPLIES AND MATERIALS

Crayons
Record player/tape recorder/CD player
Records, tapes, or CDs with different tempos
Butcher paper

PREPARATION

None

ACTIVITY

Tape the butcher paper to the table. Set the record player on a nearby shelf. Start the music. As each child wants to color, give him a crayon. Encourage the children to *"listen"* to the music and *"color"* to the beat of the music -- if the music is fast, they can color fast; if the music is slow, they can color slowly; if the music sounds like marching, they could make their crayons march; and so on.

HINT: Children do not need much direction. Their crayons move very naturally to the different tempos.

SUN CRAYON RECIPE

SUPPLIES AND MATERIALS

Old crayons
Cookie sheet or brownie pan
Variety of molds, such as:
- Styrofoam egg cartons
- Aluminum foil cupcake liners
- Disposable cups
- Ice cube trays
- Popsicle molds
- Candy molds

MAKE THE SUN CRAYONS

1. Let the children help you peel the paper wrappings off the crayons.

2. Break the crayons into small pieces.

3. Choose one or more molds, and put the crayon pieces in them, filling each one half to three-fourths full. (Make multi-color or one-color crayons.)

4. Put the mold/s on a tray. Set the tray in the sun to let the crayons melt.

5. Leave the tray out overnight so the crayons harden.

6. In the morning pop out the new crayons!

STORE THE CRAYONS

Keep the crayons in a resealable bag.

SUN CRAYON FENCE SCRIBBLE

SIZE OF GROUP: Small or large group
DO THE ACTIVITY: Outside

SUPPLIES AND MATERIALS

Sun crayons (See recipe page 40)
Large piece of cardboard
Clothespins

PREPARATION

☞ Cut off the side of an appliance box.

ACTIVITY

Use clothespins to hang the cardboard on the fence.
Have the bag of SUN CRAYONS in your pocket. When a child wants to color on the cardboard, give him a crayon or let him choose his own from the bag. Let the children *"scribble and color"* all over the cardboard for as long as each would like.

HINT: If one side gets filled with color, have the children help you turn it over, and then re-hang it. Now the children are set to scribble all over the second side.

CRAYON MURALS

SIZE OF GROUP: Small group
DO THE ACTIVITY: On Back of a Cabinet

SUPPLIES AND MATERIALS

8-10 crayons
String
Butcher paper

PREPARATION

☞ String Each Crayon.

1. Use a plastic knife and cut a notch around the top of the crayon.

2. Tie a 2-4 foot piece of string in the notch.

3. Repeat the process for the other crayons. (Make several strings extra long, so they hang to the bottom of your cabinet.)

☞ Cut the butcher paper to fit the back of a cabinet.

ACTIVITY

Tape the butcher paper to the back of a cabinet. Firmly tape the strings along the top of the cabinet, so the crayons hang along the entire length of the paper. Let the children use the crayons to *"scribble"* over the entire sheet.

Leave the paper up until it is filled with color and then hang it in a prominent place for everyone to see.

CRAYON DOTS

SIZE OF GROUP: Small or large group
DO THE ACTIVITY: At the Art Table

SUPPLIES AND MATERIALS

Crayons
Easel paper

PREPARATION

None

ACTIVITY

Tape several pieces of paper to the table.
When the children want to color, give them a crayon. After several children have gathered, you take a crayon and begin chanting *"dot, dot, dot, dot..."* as you make dots on the paper. The children who want to, will join you and start to make their dots as they chant *"dot, dot, dot...."*

VARIATION

MORE CRAYONING
Instead of chanting *"dot, dot, dot...,"* chant:

- ☛ *"Line, line, line..."*
- ☛ *"Curve, curve, curve..."*
- ☛ *"Circle, circle, circle..."*
- ☛ *"Fast, fast, fast..."*
- ☛ *"Slow, slow, slow..."*

MORE DOTS
Instead of using crayons, use colored markers or pencils and make more dots, curves, lines, zig-zags, and swirls.

CHUNKY CRAYON RECIPE

SUPPLIES AND MATERIALS

Old crayons
Muffin tins
Warming tray/oven

MAKE THE CRAYONS

1. Have the children help you peel the paper wrapping off the old crayons and break the crayons into small pieces.

2. Fill the muffin cups about half full of crayon pieces.

3. If You Are Using An Oven:
    ☛ Turn the oven on very low. After it has warmed up, set the muffin tin on a rack. Let the crayons melt and then turn off the oven.

   If You Are Using A Warming Tray:
    ☛ Turn the warming tray on medium or high. Set the muffin tin on the warming tray. Let the crayons melt and then turn off the warming tray.

4. Let the crayons sit in the oven or on the warming tray overnight until they harden. Pop your new crayons out of the muffin cups!

STORE THE CRAYONS

Keep the crayons in a resealable bag.

CHUNKY CRAYON SCRIBBLE

SIZE OF GROUP: Small group
DO THE ACTIVITY: In the Water Table

SUPPLIES AND MATERIALS

Chunky crayons (See recipe on page 44)
Solid color shelf paper or wallpaper

PREPARATION

☛ Cut several sheets of paper to fit in your water table.

ACTIVITY

Put a sheet of paper in the water table. Let the children use the CHUNKY CRAYONS and *"scribble"* for as long as they would like. When one paper is filled with color, hang it on a wall near the table. Set another sheet of paper in the water table and let the children continue to scribble.

EXTENSION

SCRIBBLE AND FINGERPAINT
On the next day tape the CHUNKY CRAYON SCRIBBLES to the art table and let the children fingerpaint on them. As they are fingerpainting, talk about how the *"crayon scribbles"* feel.

CRAYON CARS

lines ~ curves

SIZE OF GROUP: Individual or small group
DO THE ACTIVITY: At the Art Table

SUPPLIES AND MATERIALS

Crayons
Large-type miniature cars
Masking tape
Shelf paper

PREPARATION

☛ Make the Crayon Cars

1. Stand a crayon in the front or back of a car.

2. Wind a piece of tape around the car several times, so the crayon is firmly attached.

3. Repeat the process for each car.

4. Park the CRAYON CARS in a box.

ACTIVITY

Tape the shelf paper to the table. Have the cars nearby.

Give the children CRAYONS CARS and let them each drive their cars back and forth along the shelf paper road. As the children are driving, talk about their vehicles.

"Geraldo, your car is making a very straight line."

"Ti, look at the squiggly line your red car is making."

"Mary, can you make your green car curve back and forth?"

"Cheryl, your car is going very fast!"

BODY TRACINGS

SIZE OF GROUP: Individual children
DO THE ACTIVITY: On the Floor

SUPPLIES AND MATERIALS

Chunky crayons
Newsprint or butcher paper

PREPARATION

None

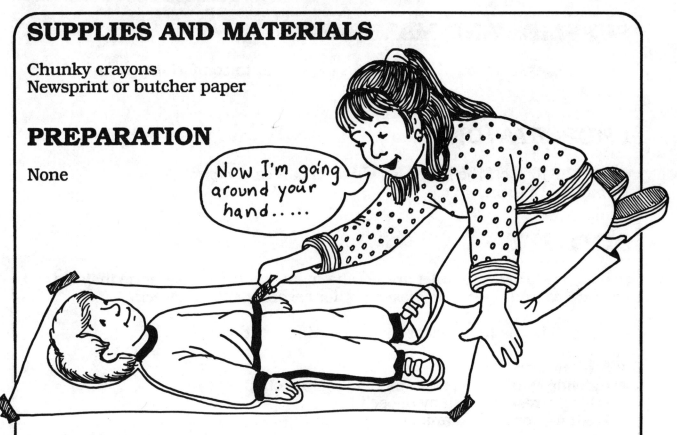

ACTIVITY

Roll out the paper on the floor.

Have a child lie down. Using a chunky crayon, trace his body. As you are tracing, talk about the body parts you are going around. For example:

"I am starting at your head, Eric, and going down to your shoulder, along your arm...." Continue until you get back to where you began.

After you've finished each child, *"cut out"* the tracing, and let the child *"color"* himself.

Hang all the tracings in the hall for everyone to see.

SIT AND SCRIBBLE

SIZE OF GROUP: Individual child
DO THE ACTIVITY: Anyplace in the room

SUPPLIES AND MATERIALS

Sturdy boxes, each one large enough for a child to comfortably sit in
Crayons

PREPARATION

☛ Cut the tops off the boxes, so children can easily climb in
and out of them.

ACTIVITY

Set several boxes in a quiet area of the room. Let a child sit or lie inside a
box and color it. Leave the boxes out for several days to a week.

After each box is full of color, use it for different things:

☛ Storing toys
☛ Individual activities, such as reading to a child,
taking a rest, playing by oneself
☛ Push toy for stuffed animals.

COLORED TUBES

SIZE OF GROUP: Small group
DO THE ACTIVITY: At the art table

SUPPLIES AND MATERIALS

Crayons
Large, sturdy tubes such as those from butcher paper
Butcher paper
Masking tape

PREPARATION

☞ Cut a piece of butcher paper to fit on your art table.

ACTIVITY

Tape butcher paper to the art table. Tape several tubes firmly to the butcher paper. Set the crayons on the table.

Let the children *"scribble"* all over the tubes and paper for as long as each would like.

EXTENSION

Use the colored tubes to play games with the children:

☞ **WHERE'S THE BLOCK?** Stand the tube straight up on the floor. Drop a block down the tube. Ask *"Where's the block?"* Let the child find it. Play again and again.

☞ **HERE COMES THE BALL.** Lay the tube on the floor. You sit at one end and a child sits at the other end. Roll a ball through the tube and let the child catch it. She rolls it back to you. Continue.

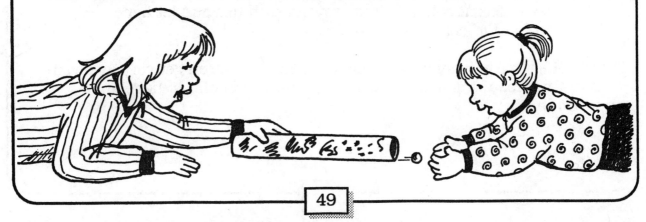

CRAYON MELT

smear

SIZE OF GROUP: Individual children
DO THE ACTIVITY: In a Quiet Area of the Room

SUPPLIES AND MATERIALS

Chubby crayons
Warming tray
Aluminum foil
Mittens

PREPARATION

☞ Peel the paper wrapping off the crayons.
(The children can help you do this. It is
a great small motor activity.)

ACTIVITY

Put the warming tray on a table near an
electrical outlet. After plugging it in, tape
the cord down so no-one trips over it.

When a child wants to color, tape a piece
of aluminum foil to the warming tray.
As you are taping the foil, have the child put on
mittens. Hand the child a crayon or let her choose one.

Encourage her to slowly move the crayon over the foil, watching
the crayon melt as she goes. After awhile, ask her if she would
like to use a different color. Switch crayons with her and let her
continue to *"smear"* color on the foil.

HINT: Offer this activity several days in a row. Children get very involved
with it, thus requiring more than one day for each child to have an
opportunity.

CRAYON RUBBINGS

SIZE OF GROUP: Any size group
DO THE ACTIVITY: Outside

SUPPLIES AND MATERIALS

Old crayons
Lightweight paper

PREPARATION

☛ Peel the paper off all
the crayons. Put them
in a bag or box.

ACTIVITY

Bring the paper and crayons
outside. Put them on a small
table in a shady area. Let the
children color when they want to.

Sit with the children while they
are coloring, and show them how
to use crayons on their sides.
Extend this activity to other
areas of the playground, and do
rubbings with those who want to.
Use things which are firm and
have good texture. For example:

☛ Cement
☛ Side of building
☛ Fence
☛ Stones
☛ Tree bark
☛ Table tops
☛ Steps on the slide

HINT: Children really like to scribble with the tips of their crayons. Using
them on their sides is difficult. Children need lots of opportunities.

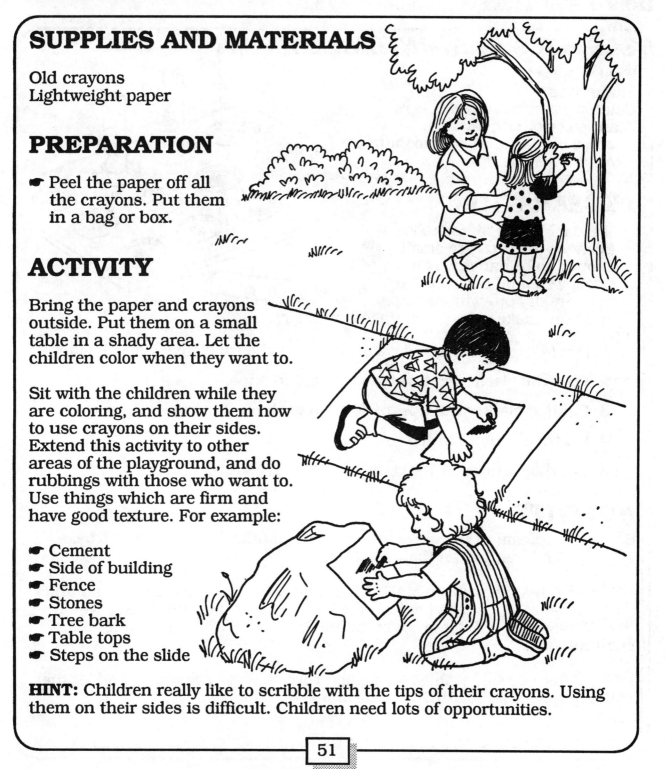

MARKER SCRIBBLE

scribble ~ dot

SIZE OF GROUP: Individuals or small group
DO THIS ACTIVITY: In the Water Table

SUPPLIES AND MATERIALS

Plaster of Paris
Muffin tins
Colored water-soluble markers
Giant piece or several large
  pieces of thick, flat styrofoam to fit
  in the water table

PREPARATION

☛ Make a Marker Storage Tin.
Because the caps are small
enough to be dangerous if
swallowed, and because the
markers dry out without caps
on them, make a special storage container.

1. Mix Plaster of Paris and water until it is the consistency of cake mix.

2. Pour the plaster mixture into the muffin cups.

3. Put one marker cap upside-down in each muffin cup.

4. Let the mixture harden.

5. Put the markers in the caps.

ACTIVITY

Set the styrofoam in the water table. Set the marker storage tin nearby. Have the children put on their smocks.

When the children want to MARKER SCRIBBLE, give each of them a marker and let them *"scribble and dot"* on the styrofoam for as long as they would like. If they want a different color, switch markers with them and let them continue.

HINT: After one side is filled with color, turn the styrofoam over and let the children MARKER SCRIBBLE some more.

MARKER ON FABRIC

SIZE OF GROUP: Small or large group
DO THIS ACTIVITY: At the Art Table

SUPPLIES AND MATERIALS

Colored water-soluble markers in the
 MARKER STORAGE TIN (See
 directions page 52)
Large piece of fabric,
 such as a bedsheet

PREPARATION

None

ACTIVITY

Tape the fabric tightly to the table. Have the children put on their smocks.

Let the children use different colored markers to *"scribble"* over the entire
piece of fabric. Encourage them to use big arm movements, long lines, and
so on. After a child is finished with his marker, hold the marker storage tin
for him, and let him stick his marker back into the cap.

EXTENSION

USE THE DECORATED FABRIC
After the fabric has dried, use it with the children:

- ☛ Tablecloth for snack
- ☛ Picnic blanket for outside.

- ☛ Tent over the climber

PENCIL SCRIBBLE

scribble ~ dot

SIZE OF GROUP: Any size group
DO THE ACTIVITY: At the Art Table

SUPPLIES AND MATERIALS

Wallpaper
Carpenter pencils

PREPARATION

None

ACTIVITY

Tape the wallpaper rightside-down to the art table.

When a child wants to PENCIL SCRIBBLE, let her choose a pencil and then *"scribble and dot"* all over the paper for as long as she wants.

HINT: Encourage the children to use all sides of their pencils. They are really different, and children can make lots of new strokes with them. All they need is a little encouragement.

Art Table

DOODLE AROUND

scribble ~ smear

SIZE OF GROUP: Small or large group
DO THE ACTIVITY: At the Art Table

SUPPLIES AND MATERIALS

Butcher paper
Colored water-soluble markers
Colored pencils
Chalk
Crayons
Tempera paint
Easel brushes

PREPARATION

None

ACTIVITY

This is a Progressive Art Activity.

Tape the butcher paper to the art table. Have the children put on their smocks.

Each day the children can *"scribble and smear"* on the same paper, using a different art medium.

Day 1 -- Have the children use crayons to scribble on the paper.

Day 2 -- Have the children use colored pencils on the same piece of paper they used the previous day.

Day 3 -- Use markers to continue scribbling and smearing on the same sheet of paper.

Day 4 -- Let the children use paint and brushes to smear color all over the mural.

Day 5 -- Finish the mural with colored chalk.

Hang this DOODLE AROUND Mural in a special place for everyone to enjoy looking at and talking about.

Using Doughs

CLOUD DOUGH RECIPE

SUPPLIES AND MATERIALS

1 cup vegetable oil
6 cups flour
1 cup water
Food coloring (optional)

MAKE THE DOUGH

1. Add the food coloring to the water.

2. Put the flour and oil into a large bowl.

3. Slowly add the water, stirring as you pour. Continue mixing the ingredients until you get a soft dough. Add a little more water or flour if necessary.

4. Put the dough on the table and knead it until it is completely blended. (This dough will have a very oily texture.)

STORE THE DOUGH

Put the dough in a covered plastic container or resealable plastic bag.

CLOUD DOUGH PLAY

poke
~
squish
~
pound

SIZE OF GROUP: Small group

DO THE ACTIVITY: In Messy Trays -- Great dough for one
child to use in a dish tub set on the floor

SUPPLIES AND MATERIALS

Cloud dough (See recipe on page 58.)

PREPARATION

None

ACTIVITY

This is a very pliable, tactile dough -- great beginning soft dough experience. Let the children put on smocks and then use their hands and fingers
to:

Squeeze	Mold	Smush
Squish	Twist	Roll
Pull	Poke	
Pound		

CORN STARCH
DOUGH RECIPE

mix ~ save

SUPPLIES AND MATERIALS

1 1/2 cups corn starch
1/2 cup water

MAKE THE DOUGH

1. Pour the cornstarch in a bowl.

2. Slowly add the water, mixing with a spoon or your fingers.

STORE THE DOUGH

This dough only lasts for several days before turning moldy. Keep it in a covered bowl or resealable bag.

CORN STARCH DOUGH PLAY

poke ~ push ~ spread

SIZE OF GROUP: Small group
DO THE ACTIVITY: In Messy Trays on tables, in Busing Tubs on the floor, at the Water Table -- great dough for young toddlers in High Chairs

SUPPLIES AND MATERIALS

Corn starch dough (See recipe on page 60.)
Large, shallow pan like a sheet cake pan

PREPARATION

None

ACTIVITY

Children love this dough. It feels so good in their hands and thus is very soothing. It also changes as they play with it. The dough literally melts in their hands when they touch it, and then becomes firmer when they leave it alone.

Put the dough in the water table or in a container. Set the container on the table or floor. Have the children put on smocks and then *"poke, push, and spread"* the dough for as long as they would like.

HINT: Easy clean-up -- wash away with water or let dry and vacuum.

VARIATIONS

COLORED CORN STARCH DOUGH.
Add food coloring to the water and make the dough. Take it outside and let the children play with it in the shade. (This colored dough stains rugs and flooring. By using it outside, you are giving your children a new experience and keeping your classroom neat.)

ADD PROPS
After the children have had lots of opportunities to play with just the dough, put out sieves, tea balls, colanders, strainers, and other objects with holes for the dough to drip through.

COOKED SOFT DOUGH RECIPE

(small portion)

SUPPLIES AND MATERIALS

1 cup flour
1/2 cup salt
1 cup water
2 T vegetable oil
1 T cream of tartar (spice shelf)

MAKE THE DOUGH

1. Put the flour, salt, oil and cream
   of tartar in a large pan.

2. Add the water.

3. Cook the ingredients over a low
   to medium heat until in forms a ball.
   Stir the dough while it is cooking.

4. When finished put it on waxed paper
   to cool. Knead the dough if necessary.

STORE THE DOUGH

Keep the dough in an airtight container.
It does not crumble and will last a
long time if stored well.

SOFT COOKED DOUGH PLAY

(small portion)

SIZE OF GROUP: Individual and small group
DO THE ACTIVITY: At the Art Table

SUPPLIES AND MATERIALS
Soft dough (See recipe on page 62.)

PREPARATION
None

ACTIVITY
Put the dough on the art table. Have the children wear smocks.

Let the children *"poke, squish, and pound"* the dough with and without props.

VARIATIONS
This is a quick, easy recipe for small amounts and thus is perfect for lots of variations.

☛ **COLORED DOUGH:** Make the recipe several times, using different colors. Simply add food coloring to the water and proceed with the recipe as described.

☛ **SMELLY DOUGH:** Make the recipe several times using different scents such as peppermint, cinnamon, or vanilla extracts, unsweetened powdered drink mixes, and unsweetened gelatin. Simply add a scent to the water, and proceed with the recipe as described.

☛ **TEXTURED DOUGH:** (Especially good for older twos.) Make the dough with different textures such as sawdust, sand, coffee grounds, and crushed egg shells. Simply stir the textured material with the dry ingredients and proceed as described.

COOKED DOUGH RECIPE

(large portion)

mix ~ save

SUPPLIES AND MATERIALS

5 cups flour
1 cup salt
4T alum (spice shelf)
2T vegetable oil
3 cups water
Food coloring (optional)

MAKE THE DOUGH

1. Boil the water. (Add food coloring to the water if you want a colored dough.)

2. Mix all of the dry ingredients and oil in a large bowl.

3. Add the boiling water. Stir together.

4. When the mixture is cool enough, put it on a table and knead it until it is thoroughly mixed.

STORE THE DOUGH

Put the dough in a tightly covered container. Keep it in the refrigerator overnight. If the dough begins to get dry, add a little water.

COOKED DOUGH PLAY
(large portion)

poke ~ squish ~ pound

SIZE OF GROUP: Small group
DO THE ACTIVITY: At the Art Table

SUPPLIES AND MATERIALS
Soft dough (See recipe on page 64.)

PREPARATION
None

ACTIVITY
Let the children *"poke, squish,* and *pound"* the dough with and without props.

Try these props:
- Plastic pizza cutters
- Garlic press
- Rolling pins (different sizes)
- Cookie cutters
- Popsicle sticks (Add the candles to the cake and sing *"Happy Birthday."*)
- Potato mashers
- Clay pounders
- Clothespins
- Biscuit cutters
- Dishes (Have a 'tea party')

NO-COOK DOUGH RECIPE

mix ~ save

SUPPLIES AND MATERIALS

2 cups flour
2T salt
2T vegetable oil
2t alum
   (from the spice shelf)
1 cup very hot water
   (safety)
Food coloring

MAKE THE DOUGH

1. Mix the flour, salt, vegetable oil, and alum in a large bowl.

2. Add the food coloring to the water.

3. Pour the colored water into the mixture in the large bowl and stir.

4. Once the dough is mixed and cool enough to touch, put it on the table and knead it until totally mixed.

STORE THE DOUGH

Keep the dough in an airtight container. This dough does not last as long as the cooked doughs, but is a great recipe to do with the children. If it begins to crumble or get dry, add a little water and knead again.

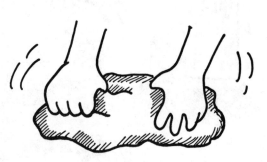

NO-COOK DOUGH PLAY

poke
~
squish
~
pound

SIZE OF GROUP: Small group
DO THE ACTIVITY: At the Art Table

SUPPLIES AND MATERIALS

No-cook soft dough (See recipe on page 66.)

PREPARATION

None

ACTIVITY

Make this dough with the children. (Keep the hot water up high or away from the activity until you need it.)

Have all of the ingredients and measuring supplies nearby. You measure each ingredient, and then let a child put it into the bowl. (Except hot water.) After all of the ingredients are in the bowl, let the children take turns mixing them together.

If you are working with toddlers or younger twos, keep the dough in the bowl and knead it. After the dough is ready, divide it into small pieces and let the children *"poke, squish, and pound"* it.

If you are working with older twos, let them knead the dough on the table and then play with it.

SILLY PUTTY RECIPE

mix
~
save

SUPPLIES AND MATERIALS

1 cup white glue
1 cup liquid starch (Sta-Flo)

MAKE THE DOUGH

1. Pour both ingredients into a large bowl.

2. Mix them together using a heavy-duty spoon or hand mixer. (This takes a little while. Be patient.) If the PUTTY is too sticky add a little more starch. If it is too thin add a little more glue.

You can make larger batches of SILLY PUTTY by simply increasing the amounts. Just remember to use equal portions of starch and glue.

STORE THE DOUGH

Put the dough in a tightly covered container or plastic bag. Keep in the refrigerator. It will be stiff and very cold each morning so plan to take a little time to knead it until it softens up.

SILLY PUTTY PLAY

SIZE OF GROUP: Small or large group
DO THE ACTIVITY: At the Art Table

SUPPLIES AND MATERIALS

Silly putty
    (See recipe on page 68.)

PREPARATION

None

ACTIVITY

Have the children put on their smocks. SILLY PUTTY is a very different *"feeling"* dough. It starts out cold and stiff each morning and becomes warm and pliable as you *"poke and squish"* it.

While playing, alert the children to the *"snapping"* sound this dough can make when they squeeze it in their fists.

Let the children pair up and slowly pull the dough apart. How far can they stretch it before it breaks?

HINT: It is very important that children wear smocks, because this dough sticks to clothing.

VARIATIONS

PASTEL PUTTY

Stir food coloring into the white glue and then mix it with the liquid starch as described in the recipe.

ADD PROPS

After children have had lots of opportunity to play and explore the PUTTY, add one or two props. Because of the consistency of this dough, cutting utensils are perfect with it. Try plastic pizza cutters, popsicle sticks, safety scissors, dull plastic knives, and dull table knives.

PEANUT BUTTER DOUGH RECIPE

(an edible dough)

SUPPLIES AND MATERIALS

1 cup low-fat peanut butter
1 cup oatmeal
1/2 cup honey
1 cup non-fat powdered milk

MAKE THE DOUGH

1. Put the oatmeal and powdered milk in a large bowl and mix them together.

2. Add the honey and peanut butter to the dry ingredients and mix them all together with a large wooden spoon.

3. Continue to mix the DOUGH until it forms one large ball.

STORE THE DOUGH

If you do not use the DOUGH right away, put it in a resealable plastic bag or airtight container. Put the DOUGH in the refrigerator until you use it.

PEANUT BUTTER DOUGH SNACK

(an edible dough)

SIZE OF GROUP: Small or large group
DO THE ACTIVITY: Anyplace in the room

SUPPLIES AND MATERIALS

Ingredients to make PEANUT BUTTER PLAYDOUGH (See recipe on page 70.)
Small spoon for each child

PREPARATION

☞ Wash and sanitize the table you will be using.

ACTIVITY

Before doing this activity, have all the children wash their hands. If
necessary have them push up the sleeves on their shirts.

Make the PEANUT BUTTER PLAYDOUGH with the children. First let them
pour the ingredients into a large bowl and then take turns stirring the
mixture. When the ingredients are almost mixed together,
stirring oftentimes becomes difficult. You might have
to finish the stirring.

Have each child use a small spoon to scoop a little
bit of DOUGH from the big ball. Let her form it
into a shape. Enjoy eating the DOUGH.

VARIATIONS
MORE PEANUT BUTTER DOUGH

Substitute other textured ingredients for the oatmeal:
  ☞ Graham cracker crumbs
  ☞ Cereals such as Kix, Rice Krispies, Cheerios
  ☞ Wheat germ
  ☞ Mashed bananas
     (eliminate the honey)

shape
~
eat

THUMBPRINT DOUGH RECIPE

(an edible dough)

SUPPLIES AND MATERIALS

2 cups of flour
1t salt
2/3 cup oil
4-5T water

MAKE THE DOUGH

1. Put the flour and salt in a large bowl and mix them together.

2. Add the oil and water.

3. Use a fork or your hands to mix the ingredients together until they form a ball.

STORE THE DOUGH

If you do not use the DOUGH right away, put it in a resealable plastic bag or airtight container. Put the DOUGH in the refrigerator until you use it.

THUMBPRINT DOUGH SNACK

(an edible dough)

SIZE OF GROUP: Small or large group
DO THE ACTIVITY: Anyplace in the room

SUPPLIES AND MATERIALS

Ingredients to make the THUMBPRINT DOUGH
(See recipe on page 72)
Cookie sheet

PREPARATION

None

ACTIVITY

Before doing this activity, have all of the children wash their hands. If necessary have them push up the sleeves on their shirts.

Make the THUMBPRINT DOUGH with the children. First let them pour the ingredients into a large bowl and then take turns stirring the mixture with their hands or a fork until it forms a large ball.

Have each child use a small spoon to scoop a little bit of DOUGH from the big ball. Let him form it into a shape and set it on a greased cookie sheet. Have him make a thumb print in his cookie.

Bake the THUMB PRINT DOUGH cookies at 325 degrees for 10 minutes. Let them cool and then fill them with peanut butter or cream cheese. Enjoy them with glasses of milk for snack or as dessert at lunch.

Using Paints

PAINTED MARBLE CRAWL

crawl ~ roll

SIZE OF GROUP: Individual children
DO THE ACTIVITY: On the Floor

SUPPLIES AND MATERIALS

Tempera paint
Margarine containers
Light colored sheets of paper
Small marbles
Several coffee cans
Spoons

PREPARATION

☛ Pour different colors of paint
into margarine containers.

☛ Place several marbles and
one spoon in each container.

ACTIVITY

Help each child loosely roll up his piece of paper and put it in the coffee can
so that it fits against the inside. Scoop 3-5 marbles out of the paint and put
them in the middle of the can. Cover the can. Tape it closed if necessary.

Let the child put the can on the floor and *"roll"* it around as he *"crawls"*
after it.

When he has finished, ask him if he would like to put more painted marbles
in the can and roll it again, or if he is finished and would like to hang up
his painting to dry.

PAINTED PEBBLE SHAKE

SIZE OF GROUP: Individual children
DO THE ACTIVITY: On the Floor

scoop ~ shake

SUPPLIES AND MATERIALS

Large clear plastic jars with wide
    lids and handles such as
    those used for dry cat food
Light colored paper
Small pebbles or marbles
Tempera paint
Margarine tubs
Spoons

PREPARATION

☞ Cut the paper to fit in the jars.

☞ Pour tempera paint in
   margarine tubs.

☞ Put pebbles and a spoon in
   each margarine tub.

ACTIVITY

Play children's favorite music on the record player.

Help each child roll up his piece of paper and put it in a plastic jar.
"Scoop" pebbles/marbles out of the paint and put them in the jar. Screw
the top tightly on the jar.

Let the children *"shake"* the bottles as the music plays. When each child
finishes, let him help you take the paper out of the bottle, unroll it, and
look at the design the painted pebbles made on his paper. Hang up.

VARIATION
MORE PAINTED PEBBLE SHAKE
Instead of using the large bottles with handles, use containers
which have no handles, such as wide-mouth plastic peanut butter
containers or heavy cardboard cylinder boxes for cereal and chips.

MARBLE ROLL AROUND

SIZE OF GROUP: Individual children
DO THE ACTIVITY: Anyplace in the room

SUPPLIES AND MATERIALS

Tempera paint
Marbles
Dish tubs/sturdy boxes
Construction paper

PREPARATION

☛ Pour the tempera paint into margarine tubs. Add a spoon to each tub.

☛ Put several marbles in each tub/box.

ACTIVITY

Before each child begins this activity, have him push up his sleeves.

Have a child take a piece of construction paper and lay it in the bottom of a dish tub. Let him put several marbles in the paint. "*Scoop*" the marbles out of the paint for him (or do it together) and put them in the tub/box. Encourage him to "*roll*" the marbles around, making trails all over his paper. Let him re-dip his marbles and roll them around again. He may want to try another color or several colors at one time.

VARIATIONS

MORE DIFFICULT

After children are able to control the marbles, let them MARBLE PAINT on rectangular paper cut in shoe box tops and circular paper cut for pie pans.

GOLF BALL ROLL

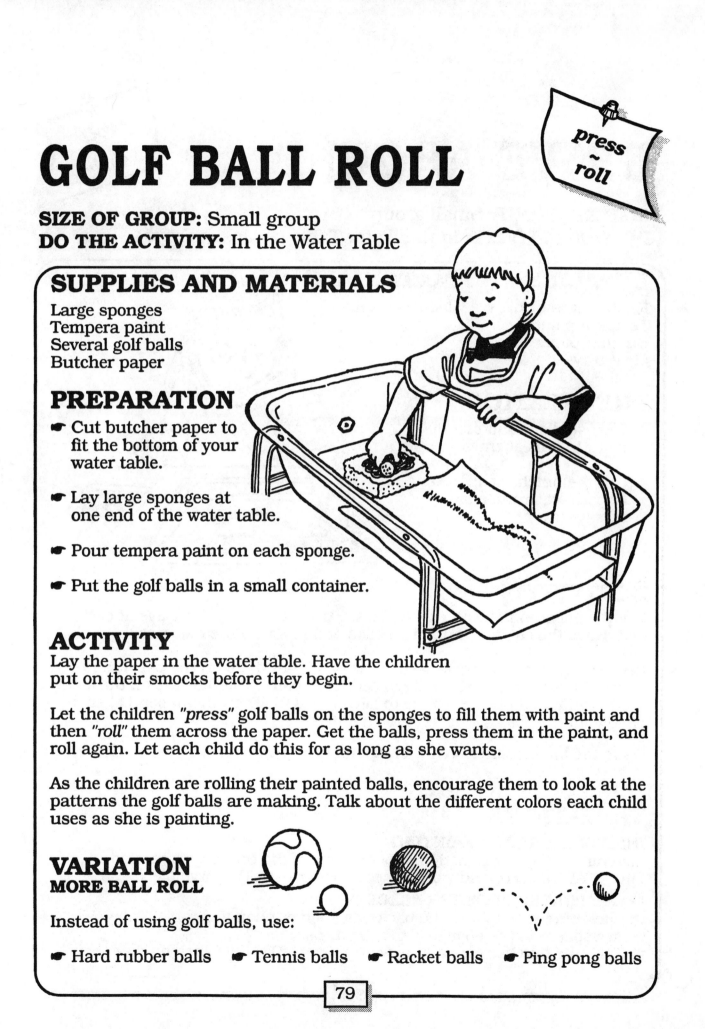

press ~ roll

SIZE OF GROUP: Small group
DO THE ACTIVITY: In the Water Table

SUPPLIES AND MATERIALS

Large sponges
Tempera paint
Several golf balls
Butcher paper

PREPARATION

☛ Cut butcher paper to fit the bottom of your water table.

☛ Lay large sponges at one end of the water table.

☛ Pour tempera paint on each sponge.

☛ Put the golf balls in a small container.

ACTIVITY

Lay the paper in the water table. Have the children put on their smocks before they begin.

Let the children *"press"* golf balls on the sponges to fill them with paint and then *"roll"* them across the paper. Get the balls, press them in the paint, and roll again. Let each child do this for as long as she wants.

As the children are rolling their painted balls, encourage them to look at the patterns the golf balls are making. Talk about the different colors each child uses as she is painting.

VARIATION
MORE BALL ROLL

Instead of using golf balls, use:

☛ Hard rubber balls   ☛ Tennis balls   ☛ Racket balls   ☛ Ping pong balls

79

DRIVE AROUND

roll ~ drive

SIZE OF GROUP: Small group
DO THE ACTIVITY: In the Water Table or Messy Trays

SUPPLIES AND MATERIALS

Rubber cars with large wide-tread tires
Tempera paint
Butcher paper
Meat trays

PREPARATION

☛ Pour shallow amounts of paint in 2 meat trays.

☛ Cut the butcher paper to fit your water table or messy tray.

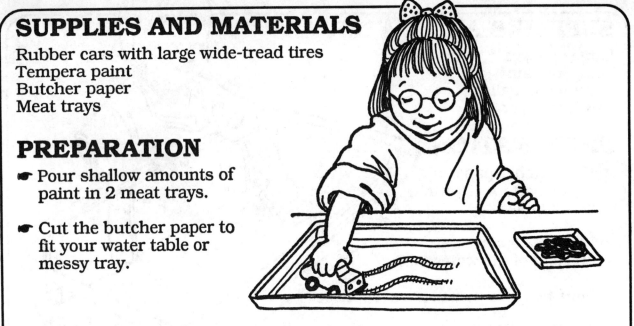

ACTIVITY

Lay the paper in the water table/messy tray. Set the paint trays at each end. Have the children put on smocks and push up their sleeves.

Let the children *"roll"* their cars in the paint, set them on the paper, and *"drive"* them around. When they need more paint, roll the cars on the meat trays again, and then continue to DRIVE AROUND on the paper. Let each child continue for as long as he would like.

Hang the large banner on a wall, door, or bulletin board.

VARIATIONS

INDIVIDUAL TRACK PAINTING
Let children lay construction paper on top of the butcher paper and DRIVE AROUND on individual sheets rather than the large piece.

MAKE TRACKS IN OTHER PLACES
☛ Tack butcher paper to the back of a shelf or changing table. Tape newspaper to the floor to catch the drips.
☛ Tack the butcher paper on a wall, fence, or storage shed outside.

TEXTURED ROLLER PAINTING

SIZE OF GROUP: Small group
DO THE ACTIVITY: In the Water Table or Messy Trays

SUPPLIES AND MATERIALS

Wallpaper or ink rollers
Masking tape
Butcher paper
Large sponges
Tempera paint

PREPARATION

☛ Cut butcher paper to fit in the bottom of your water table/messy tray.

☛ Dampen the sponges and put each one on a meat tray. Pour a different colored paint on each sponge.

☛ Wrap masking tape around the rollers in various patterns.

ACTIVITY

Lay the butcher paper in the water table/messy tray. Set the paint trays and textured rollers in the corners. Have the children put on their smocks and push up their sleeves before they begin to ROLLER PAINT.

Help each child move his roller back and forth several times over one of the painted sponges. Then let him *"roll"* it on the butcher paper with short, long, curved, and wiggly strokes. Encourage the children to roll their rollers in the paint each time they run out. They may want to use the same color or a different one.

VARIATION
OTHER ROLLING PINS

Use other types of rolling pins such as:
☛ Cheese slicer without the cutting wire
☛ All sizes of paint rollers
☛ Corner paint rollers
☛ Different size pastry rolling pins -- wrap rubber bands around them.

THUMB AND FINGER DOTS

SIZE OF GROUP: Small or large group
DO THIS ACTIVITY: At the Art Table

SUPPLIES AND MATERIALS

Wide masking tape
Finger paint
Paper towels

PREPARATION

☞ Make several *"paint pads"* by folding paper towels to fit in meat trays. Pour paint on the paper towels.

ACTIVITY

Tape a long strip of masking tape on each long side of the art table. Set the paint pads near the strips. Remind the children to put on their smocks.

Let the children *"press"* their thumbs and fingers on the paint pads and then *"print"* along the tape. After each strip is filled with prints, pull it off and tape it to one of the doors in the classroom. Replace the strip with a clean one and let the children continue to FINGER AND THUMB PRINT.

HINT: Many children will want to *"smear"* with the paint on their thumbs and fingers rather than *"print"* with it. That is OK. You can encourage them to *"print"* by saying something like, *"Look, your fingerprints look like dots!"* or *"Let's make raindrops all over the tape."*

DEODORANT BOTTLE PAINTING

SIZE OF GROUP: Small group
DO THE ACTIVITY: At the Art Table

SUPPLIES AND MATERIALS

Empty deodorant bottles with roller-ball tops
Tempera paint
Newsprint, newspaper, or manilla paper

PREPARATION

☛ Take the roller-ball off the top of each bottle.
Clean the bottles and the roller-balls thoroughly.

☛ Fill the bottles with different colors of tempera
paint and replace the roller-balls.

ACTIVITY

Tape paper to the art table. Remind the
children to put on their smocks.

Let the children *"roll"* the deodorant bottles
to draw scribbles, designs, and pictures.
As they are rolling, talk about:
    ☛ The color/s they are using.
    ☛ The types of lines they are making.
    ☛ How they are moving their arms to make lines over the paper.

VARIATIONS

TWO-FISTED PAINTING
Encourage the children to paint with a roller bottle in each hand.

OTHER ROLLER BALLS
Use other types of roller-balls such as:
    ☛ Different size deodorant bottles
    ☛ Chair and table castors
    ☛ Perfume bottles

PAINT DAUBING

SIZE OF GROUP: Individual children
DO THE ACTIVITY: At the Art Table

SUPPLIES AND MATERIALS

Thick sponges or polyester batting
Tempera paint
Meat trays
Light-weight fabric, such as an
  old pillow case
String or rubber bands
Newspaper

PREPARATION

☛ Make Different Colored Paint Pads. To make each one:
    1. Put a damp sponge on a large meat tray.
    2. Pour a little tempera paint on the sponge.
    3. Gently squeeze the sponge to absorb the paint.
    4. Add a little more paint if necessary.

☛ Make Lots of Daubers. To make each one:
    1. Cut an 8" square piece of fabric.
    2. Cut a 2" square piece of thick sponge.
    3. Put the sponge or a large wad of polyester
       batting in the middle of the fabric.
    4. Gather-up the corners of the fabric and tie
       them together with string or a rubber band.

☛ Cut the newspaper into appropriate size pieces.

ACTIVITY

Tape the newspaper to the art table. Put the different colored paint pads on
the table. Set several daubers on each paint pad. Have the children put on
their smocks and push up their sleeves.

Have the children *"press"* their daubers on the paint pads and *"daub"* dots
all over their newspaper. Encourage them to change colors or refill their first
daubers and make more dots. Let them daub for as long as they want.

HINT: Refill the pads as necessary.
☛ Many children will want to *"smear"* with their daubers instead of *"daub"*
  with them. One way to encourage daubing is to have each child chant
  "dot, dot,dot, dot, dot, dot" as she paints.

SPOOL DOTTING

press~
dot~
roll

SIZE OF THE GROUP: Individual or pairs of children
DO THE ACTIVITY: At the Art Table

SUPPLIES AND MATERIALS

Wooden, plastic, or styrofoam spools
4 to 6 plastic baby-wipe boxes
Paper towels
Tempera paint
Several large corrugated boxes

PREPARATION

☞ Make Different Colored Paint Pad
Boxes. To make each one:
1. Open the baby-wipe box.

2. Fold several paper towels and
set them on one side of the box.

3. Pour paint over the paper towels.

4. Close the box so the paint pad stays
moist until you are ready to use it.

☞ Cut the corrugated box into pieces which
individual and/or pairs of children can easily use.

ACTIVITY

Put the paint pad boxes on the table. Set several spools on the empty side
of each box. Have the children put on their smocks and push up their
sleeves before they begin to paint.

When children want to SPOOL DOT, tape cardboard to the table. Let them
"press" spools in the paint and make *"dots"* all over the cardboard.

HINTS:
☞ Some children may want to press and daub with a partner, while others
would like to do it alone. Encourage the children to press and daub for
as long as they want, using different size spools and a variety of colors.

☞ Remember to keep the paint pads filled with tempera paint. This activity
needs very moist paint pads so that paint easily sticks to the spools.

STAMPS AND PADS

press ~ stamp

SIZE OF THE GROUP: Small or large group
DO THE ACTIVITY: At the Art Table

SUPPLIES AND MATERIALS

Stamps
Stamp pads
Ink refills
Shelf paper

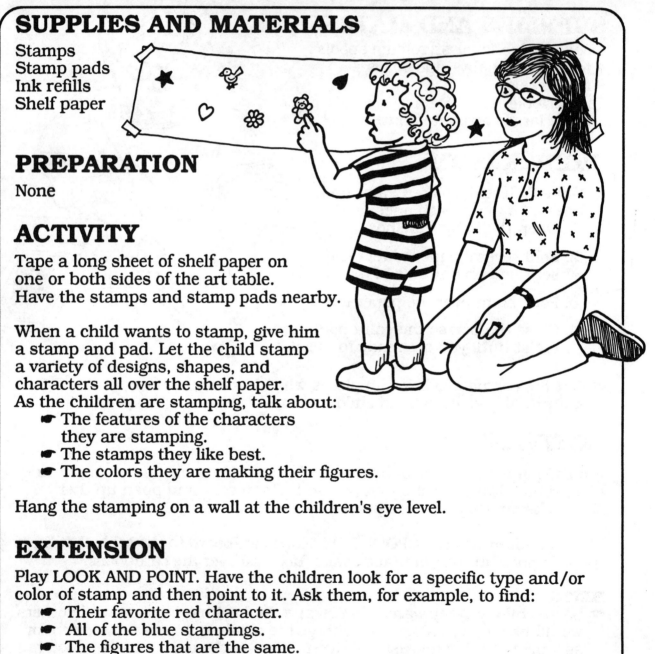

PREPARATION

None

ACTIVITY

Tape a long sheet of shelf paper on one or both sides of the art table. Have the stamps and stamp pads nearby.

When a child wants to stamp, give him a stamp and pad. Let the child stamp a variety of designs, shapes, and characters all over the shelf paper. As the children are stamping, talk about:
- ☛ The features of the characters they are stamping.
- ☛ The stamps they like best.
- ☛ The colors they are making their figures.

Hang the stamping on a wall at the children's eye level.

EXTENSION

Play LOOK AND POINT. Have the children look for a specific type and/or color of stamp and then point to it. Ask them, for example, to find:
- ☛ Their favorite red character.
- ☛ All of the blue stampings.
- ☛ The figures that are the same.
- ☛ All the green circles.

BINGO BLOTTERS

stamp

SIZE OF GROUP: Individual children
DO THE ACTIVITY: In the Water Table

SUPPLIES AND MATERIALS

Different colored bingo blotters
Wide adding machine paper

PREPARATION

None

ACTIVITY

Tape several long strips of adding
machine paper to the bottom of the
water table. Have the bingo blotters
handy. Remind the children to
put on smocks.

Let the children use different colored
blotters to *"stamp"* lots and lots of
colored dots on the narrow paper.

After each strip is filled with dots, hang it at the children's eye level on
your classroom door. Soon your door will be one of the most colorful
parts of the room.

HINT: Many children will want to *"smear"* with their blotters instead of
"stamp" with them. Remember that this is fine. However, to help learn how
to *"stamp"* with the blotters, let them pretend to be making raindrops.

VARIATIONS

WET PAPER
Use fingerpaint paper. Let the children paint their paper with water and
then use any type of blotter and *"let it pour raindrops"* all over the paper.

OTHER BLOTTERS
Clean and use other types of blotters such as shoe polish bottles with the
built-in sponge brushes. Pop the sponge off each bottle, fill it with watered-
down tempera paint, and then snap the sponge back on.

BOX PAINTING

paint

SIZE OF GROUP: Small group
DO THE ACTIVITY: Outside

SUPPLIES AND MATERIALS

Large grocery box or appliance box
Tempera paint
Juice cans
Wide brushes
Plastic pool

PREPARATION

☛ Pour several different colors of tempera paint into 5-6 juice cans. Put the cans in a cardboard soda pop carrier.

ACTIVITY

Carry the supplies outside. Set the large box in the middle of the plastic pool, and the paint and brushes next to it. Have the children put on their smocks before they begin.

As the children want to take a break from active play, let them stand in the pool and paint the box.

HINT: You may want the children to take off their shoes and socks before painting. This will keep the excess sand, dirt, etc. out of the pool.

MASHERS, FORKS, SPATULAS

SIZE OF GROUP: Small or large group
DO THE ACTIVITY: At the Art Table

SUPPLIES AND MATERIALS

Several types of utensils such as:
    Different sizes and
       shapes of spatulas
    Potato mashers with
       different designs
    Forks with different
       prongs
Old, light-colored bedsheet
Tempera paint
Sponge-type paint pads

PREPARATION

☞ Make different colored paint pads. (See directions on page 86.)

ACTIVITY

Tape the bedsheet to the art table. Put the paint pads and the utensils on the sheet. Have the children put on smocks.

Have the children *"press"* the utensils on the paint pads and then *"print"* on the sheet. Let them continue for as long as they want.

Let the sheet dry overnight. Use it the next day for a tablecloth.

VARIATIONS
OTHER UTENSILS

Use other utensils to add even more variety to this activity. Try:
    ☞ Plastic pizza cutters   ☞ Apple slicers   ☞ Biscuit cutters
    ☞ Slotted spoons   ☞ Flat strainers

BERRY BASKETS

SIZE OF GROUP: Small group
DO THE ACTIVITY: At the Art Table

SUPPLIES AND MATERIALS

Plastic berry baskets
Large, shallow paint
  containers, such as
  styrofoam produce trays
Tempera paint
Construction paper

PREPARATION

☛ Pour different colors of
  paint into the containers.

ACTIVITY

Have the children put on smocks
and push up their sleeves.

Have each child pick a piece of construction paper and set it on the table.
Tape it down for him. Let him *"press"* a berry basket in the paint and *"print"*
designs on his paper. Repeat as often as he would like using different colors
and baskets.

HINTS:

☛ Encourage the children to hold their baskets around the top edge.

☛ Have small plastic baskets with handles available for children having
  difficulty holding the berry baskets or for those who would like variety.

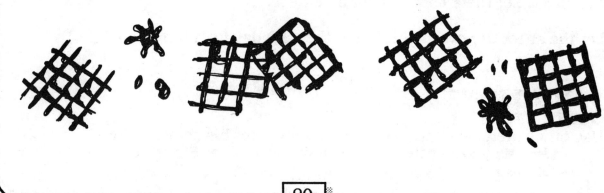

SNOW PAINTING

dip ~ paint

SIZE OF GROUP: Any size
DO THE ACTIVITY: Outside

SUPPLIES AND SUPPLIES

Food coloring
Stubby paint brushes
Several plastic milk bottles with tops
Margarine containers

PREPARATION

☛ Let the children help you make
colored water:
1. Pour clear water into a milk bottle.

2. Squeeze several drops of food
coloring into the water.
Put the top on the bottle.

3. Let the children take turns helping
you shake the bottle. Watch the clear
water turn into colored water.

4. Repeat for other colors.

ACTIVITY

Take the bottle/s of colored water, margarine containers, and brushes
outside.

When a child wants to SNOW PAINT, give her a brush and a container with
a little colored water. Have her set the container in the snow, and then
"paint" the snow for as long as she wants.

VARIATION

Make giant snowballs, build snow characters, form snow figures, etc.
"Paint" these special snow sculptures with colored water.

SPONGES AND FOAM

SIZE OF GROUP: Small group
DO THE ACTIVITY: In Messy Trays

SUPPLIES AND MATERIALS

Thick sponges and/or
  foam rubber
Wide-diameter dowel rods
Tempera paint
Large, shallow
  paint containers
Large, corrugated
  box or cardboard
Hot glue gun

PREPARATION

☛ Make the Sponge Shapes.
  To make each one:
  1. Cut the sponge/foam into a small piece.
  2. Cut a small hole in the middle of the sponge.
  3. Cut a 3" piece off the dowel rod.
  4. Using a hot glue gun, glue the dowel rod into the hole.

☛ Pour different colors of paint into the containers.

☛ Cut the corrugated box into individual pieces for one child or a pair of
  children to sponge paint on.

ACTIVITY

Put one or two paint containers on each messy tray. Have the children put
on smocks and push up their sleeves.

When each child wants to paint, tape a piece of cardboard in a messy tray
and hand him a sponge shape. Let the child *"press"* the sponges in the paint
and *"print"* lots of designs on the cardboard.

After the paintings have dried hang them from the ceiling.

HINT: Remember, many of your children will want to *"smear"* instead of
"print" with their sponges. This is OK. To help them print, you could chant,
"dot, dot, dot, dot..." as they paint.

SWATTER PAINTING

dip
~
slap

SIZE OF GROUP: Small or large group
DO THE ACTIVITY: Outside

SUPPLIES AND MATERIALS

Clean fly swatters
Pie pans
Tempera paint
Butcher paper

PREPARATION

☛ Pour shallow amounts of different colors of paint into pie pans.

☛ Cut a long piece of butcher paper and roll it up to take outside.

☛ If you don't have quick access to fly swatters, make your own.
   Get wire hangers and old nylons. To make:
   1. Pull the hanger into a diamond shape.
   2. Pull the nylon over the diamond and tie it to the handle.
   3. Tape the handle for safety.

ACTIVITY

Roll out the butcher paper in a secluded area of the playground. Put a brick on each corner of the paper to hold it down. Set the pie pans of paint around the edges of the paper. Set a fly swatter next to each one.

Let the children *"dip"* the fly swatters in the paint and *"slap"* them on the paper. Slap again and again making lots of prints. Dip the fly swatters in the paint again and print some more.

Leave the activity set up while you are outside. When it is time to go inside, leave the mural there to dry. After it is dry, gently bring it inside and hang it low on a wall for everyone to look at. If weather permits, hang it on your outside fence.

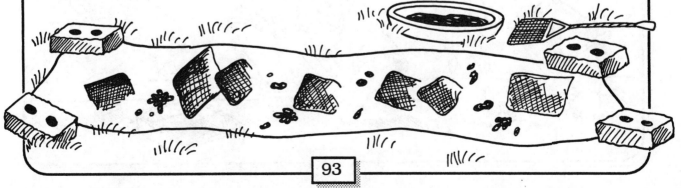

BIG BRUSH PAINTING

SIZE OF GROUP: Small group
DO THE ACTIVITY: At the Art Table

SUPPLIES AND MATERIALS

Tempera paint
Variety of big brushes
Butcher paper
Large, shallow containers such as a brownie pan

PREPARATION

☞ Pour small amounts of paint into the large containers.

☞ Cut a piece of butcher paper to fit the art table.

ACTIVITY

Tape the butcher paper to the art table. Put the paint and brushes near the paper. Have the children put on smocks, and push up their sleeves.

When the children want to paint, let them stand around the table, and fill the paper with strokes and smears of color.

VARIATION

Carry all the supplies outside. Lay the paper on the cement, and let the children paint while they're taking a break from more active play.

STRING PAINTING

dip ~ paint

SIZE OF GROUP: Small group
DO THE ACTIVITY: In the Water Table or Messy Tray

SUPPLIES AND MATERIALS

Large thread spools
Heavy-duty string
Tempera paint
Butcher paper

PREPARATION

☛ Cut the string into 12 inch pieces.
☛ Tie one piece of string to each spool.
☛ Pour different colors of paint into small margarine tubs.
☛ Cut a piece of butcher paper to fit on the bottom of the water table/messy tray.

ACTIVITY

Have the children put on their smocks and push up their sleeves before they begin to STRING PAINT.

Put the tubs of paint and string in the water table. Have the children hold the spools, dip the strings into the paint, and slowly pull them out. Encourage the children to drag, wiggle, and bounce their strings all around the paper.

VARIATIONS

DANCING STRINGS
Put the record player near the water table/messy tray. Set the activity up as you did above. Play the children's favorite music and let the children *"dance"* their strings to the beat.

STRING PAINT
with other types of string such as:
☛ Yarn
☛ Ribbon

OTHER HANDLES
☛ Large buttons
☛ Clothespins
☛ Tongue depressors

HAND PRINTS

SIZE OF GROUP: Small or large group
DO THE ACTIVITY: On the Wall

SUPPLIES AND MATERIALS

Butcher paper
Tempera paint

PREPARATION

☛ Pour different colors of paint into large shallow paint containers such as brownie pans or large meat trays.

ACTIVITY

Tape a long sheet of butcher paper to an empty wall at the children's eye level. Put the paint containers on a table next to the paper. Have the children put on their smocks and push their sleeves way up.

Show the children how to spread their fingers completely out and *"press"* their hands into the paint. Then let them push their painted hands on the paper to *"print."* Press and print again and again until the paper is filled with lots of colorful hands.

Ask the children if they would like you to write their names by their hand prints. If a child says *"Yes"* write his/her name with a wide marker.

HINT: Leave this activity set up for several days, so that all of the children have the opportunity to do it at least once.

96

PUZZLE PIECES

press
~
print

SIZE OF GROUP: Small group
DO THE ACTIVITY: At the Art Table

SUPPLIES AND MATERIALS

"Extra" puzzle pieces
  with handles
Tempera paint
Paper towels
Butcher paper

PREPARATION

☛ Cut the butcher paper to
  fit on the art table.

☛ Make several *"paint pads"*
  by folding paper towels to
  fit in meat trays. Pour
  paint on the paper towels.

ACTIVITY

Tape the butcher paper to the art table.
Lay the paint pads and puzzle pieces on
table. Let the children choose puzzle pieces,
"press" them on the paint pads and make
"prints" on the butcher paper. Talk about
what they are printing as they are doing it.

VARIATIONS

MORE CUTTERS

Use plastic biscuit and/or cookie cutters with handles to print more
shapes, figures, and characters.

PLACEMATS FOR SNACK TIME

Let the children use their favorite cutters to print on colored construction
paper. After they are dry, laminate or cover them with clear adhesive paper.
Use the special *"placemats"* for snack.

FOOTPRINTS

step ~ print

SIZE OF GROUP: Individual child
DO THE ACTIVITY: Outside or in a minimally travelled area of the room

SUPPLIES AND MATERIALS

Tempera paint
Several dish tubs
Shelf paper
Paper towels

PREPARATION

☛ Pour small amounts of different colors of paint into dish tubs.
☛ Cut shelf paper into 6 foot lengths - one for each child.
☛ Fill a bucket of water.

ACTIVITY

Put the paint, shelf paper, and water in the area.

Just before each child FOOTPRINTS, have him take off his shoes and socks and set them out of the way. If necessary, roll up his pant legs. Lay one sheet of shelf paper on the floor.

Have each child choose what color footprints he wants to make. Hold his hand as he *"steps"* into the dish tub, wiggles his feet in the paint, and steps out onto the paper. Encourage him to walk slowly along the paper, making *"prints"* as he goes. When he gets to the end, have him step off and sit down. Help him clean his feet and put his shoes and socks back on.

Let all of the footprints dry. Roll up each child's prints and let him take them home. Send a short note with the prints suggesting that the parents hang their child's prints on his bedroom door.

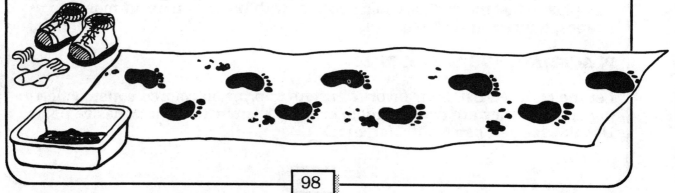

KISS THE PAPER

SIZE OF GROUP: Individual children
DO THE ACTIVITY: Anyplace in the room

SUPPLIES AND MATERIALS

Different colors of lipstick
Construction paper
Full-length mirror
Tape

PREPARATION

None

ACTIVITY

Let each child choose a piece of construction paper. Tape it to the mirror for her.

Let her choose her lipstick and then help her put it on her finger and apply it to her lips. Once the lipstick is on, let her *"kiss"* the paper as often as she'd like, making lots of lip *"prints."* Help her apply more lipstick as needed.

COLORED WATER PAINTING

SIZE OF GROUP: Small group
DO THE ACTIVITY: Outside, at the Water Table or in a Messy Tray

SUPPLIES AND MATERIALS

Butcher paper
Food coloring
Popsicle sticks

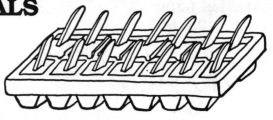

PREPARATION

☛ Make several trays of colored ice cube popsicles. To make the popsicles, pour colored water into ice cube trays and put them in the freezer. After they have partially hardened, put a popsicle stick (at a slight angle) in each one. Let them completely harden.

☛ Cut the paper to fit in your water table or messy tray.

ACTIVITY

Lay the paper in your table/tray. Pop out one tray of popsicles and put them in a pie pan. Have the children push up their sleeves.

Let the children use different popsicles to smear colored water over the paper. Replace the paper and popsicles as necessary. Clip the *"painted"* paper to your fence to dry.

HINT: Some children may want to paint with two or more popsicles at the same time.

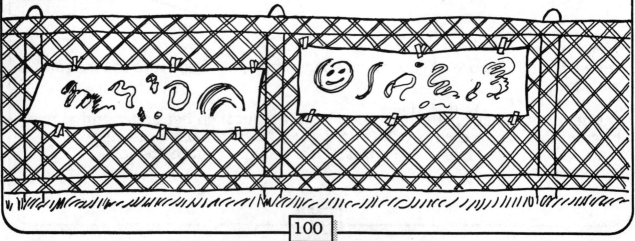

SMUSH PAINTING

drizzle ~ rub

SIZE OF GROUP: Individual children
DO THIS ACTIVITY: At the Art Table

SUPPLIES AND MATERIALS

Large construction paper
Tempera paint
Small squeeze bottles such as from white glue

- - - fold - - -

PREPARATION

☛ Pour different colors of tempera paint into the squeeze bottles.

☛ Fold all of the construction paper in half, so that one side of the paper is under the other side.

ACTIVITY

Put the folded paper and paint bottles near the table. Have the children put on smocks before doing this activity.

When each child wants to SMUSH PAINT, let him choose the paper and paint he wants to use. Have him *"drizzle"* a design on the side of the paper which is facing up.

After he has finished his design, help him carefully bring the underside out and fold it over his design, and then *"rub"* all around. As he is rubbing, say, *"smush, smush, smush...."*

Slowly open the SMUSH PAINTING and look at it together.

smush, smush, smush!

101

DRY TEMPERA

SIZE OF GROUP: Small group
DO THE ACTIVITY: Outside, in the Water Table or Messy Tray

SUPPLIES AND MATERIALS

Popsicle sticks
Salt shakers
Dry tempera paint
White butcher paper

PREPARATION

☛ Make several trays of ice cubes. After the cubes have partially hardened, put a popsicle stick (at an angle) in each one. Let them completely harden.

☛ Pour different colors of dry tempera paint in salt shakers.

☛ Cut the butcher paper to fit in the water table/messy tray.

ACTIVITY

Lay the paper in the water table/messy tray. Pop out one tray of cubes and put them in a pie pan. Set the salt shakers nearby. Have the children push up their sleeves.

When each child comes to the activity, give her a salt shaker and let her *"shake"* dry tempera paint on the paper. After she is finished shaking, have her give you the salt shaker. Let her take one or two popsicles and *"smear"* the dry paint around the paper.

VARIATION

ICICLE PAINTING
When you are outside on a cold day, break off several icicles and bring them inside. Break the icicles into small pieces (no sharp edges or points) and use them instead of ice cubes. (Remember, the children need to wear mittens while ICICLE PAINTING.)

SOAPY WATER

SIZE OF GROUP: Small group
DO THE ACTIVITY: In the Water Table

SUPPLIES AND MATERIALS

Several dishwashing sponge brushes
(The brushes in camping stores have
larger handles than the ones in grocery
stores. These handles are easier for the
younger child to hold, plus they hold
more water.)
Dish detergent
Several beach towels
Paper towels

PREPARATION

☛ Fill each dishwashing sponge about 1/4 to 1/2 full of warm water. Add
a very little detergent. Screw the top on tightly. Wrap it with tape if
necessary.

ACTIVITY

Put a cotton drop cloth or several beach towels on the floor to absorb water
that might spill over. Put the sponges in a small pail. Have the children put
on smocks and push up their sleeves as far as possible.

Let the children *"smear"* soapy water
all over the sides and bottom of the
water table. When each child
finishes washing the table,
give him a paper towel and
let him *"dry"* it.

VARIATIONS

MORE SMEARING
Fill the handles with other
liquids, such as:
☛ Water mixed with food coloring.
☛ Water mixed with dry tempera
paint.
☛ Clear water with extracts
such as peppermint or vanilla.

103

TEMPERA CAKES

dip
~
brush

SIZE OF GROUP: Small or large group
DO THE ACTIVITY: At the Art Table

SUPPLIES AND MATERIALS

Different colors of tempera paint cakes
Different width paint brushes
Construction paper

PREPARATION

☛ Pour water into small margarine tubs.

☛ Fill a dish tub about half full of water.

ACTIVITY

Have the dish tub near the activity. Put the tempera paint cakes, brushes, and containers of water on the table. Have the children put on smocks and push up their sleeves before they paint.

When each child wants to paint, help her *"dip"* her paper in the water in the dish tub. Slowly bring the paper out and lay it on the table. Let her use the brushes, different colors of tempera cakes, and water in margarine tubs to paint for as long as she would like.

CLEAR WATER

SIZE OF GROUP: Any size
DO THE ACTIVITY: Outside

SUPPLIES AND MATERIALS

Housepainting brushes
Several lightweight pails
Plastic milk bottles

PREPARATION

☛ Cut the milk bottles into buckets with handles. (See illustration.)

ACTIVITY

Help each child fill a bucket about half full of water. Give her a brush.

Let the children *"dip"* the brushes in the clear water and *"brush"* the building, playground equipment, concrete, grass, bushes, tree trunks, and benches for as long as each would like.

HINT: This is an especially good activity on a hot day. Children are often amazed at how fast the water *"disappears"* or in more scientific terms, *"evaporates."*

TOAST PAINTING SNACK

SIZE OF GROUP: Small group
DO THE ACTIVITY: Anyplace in the room near an electrical outlet.

SUPPLIES AND MATERIALS

Bread
Milk
Food coloring
Toaster
Small containers
Small brushes

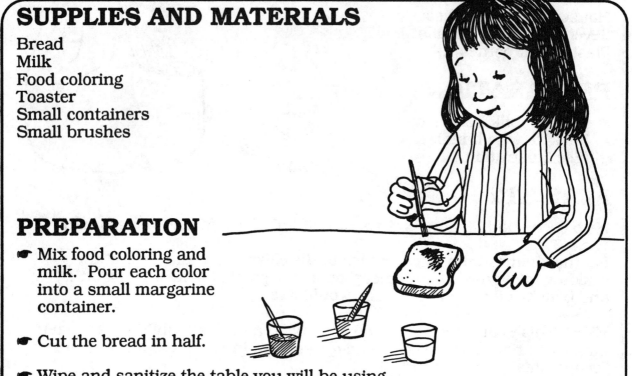

PREPARATION

☛ Mix food coloring and milk. Pour each color into a small margarine container.

☛ Cut the bread in half.

☛ Wipe and sanitize the table you will be using.

ACTIVITY

Before doing this activity, have the children wash their hands.

Put the bread, colored milk, small brushes, and toaster on a table. (Tape the toaster cord to the floor for safety.) Let the children *"brush"* their pieces of bread with colored milk. After several have finished, pop the bread into the toaster. When the pieces have popped up, let the children *"eat"* their special snack along with glasses of juice.

VARIATION
TOASTED COOKIE CUTTER PRINTS
Let the children dip cookie cutters into the colored milk and make prints on their bread. Toast the bread in toaster ovens. It is fun to watch the shapes take form as they are toasted.

COOKIE PAINTING SNACK

brush
~
eat

SIZE OF GROUP: Small or large group
DO THE ACTIVITY: Anyplace in the room

SUPPLIES AND MATERIALS

Ingredients for your children's favorite cookie recipe
4 eggs
Several drops of water
Different food colorings
Several bowls
Small brushes

PREPARATION

☛ Make the *"Cookie Paint."*

1. Separate the egg yolks and whites. Put the whites in a bowl.

2. Add several drops of water. Blend the whites and water together.

3. Separate the mixture into several small margarine tubs. Blend a different food coloring into each one.

4. Cover the *"paints"* until you're ready to use them.

☛ Wipe and sanitize the table you will be using.

ACTIVITY

Before doing this activity, have the children wash their hands.

Make your favorite cookie recipe with the children. *"Paint"* the cookies with cookie paint and small brushes, and then bake them according to the directions.

"Eat" the PAINTED COOKIES for snack after naptime.

107

LOTS OF BRUSHES

brush

LET THE CHILDREN PAINT WITH DIFFERENT, CLEAN BRUSHES

All width paint brushes
Back scrubbers
Bottle brushes
Dish brushes
Dog and cat brushes
Eye lash brushes
Eye liner brushes
Hair brushes
Lipstick brushes
Mustache brushes
Paint trim brushes -- 1/2"
Scrub brushes
Shaving cream brushes
Shoe polish applicators
Shoe shine brushes
Snow scraper brushes
Sponge brushes
Stubby handle paint brushes
Toilet bowl brushes
Toenail and fingernail brushes
Toothbrushes
Vacuum cleaner brushes

MORE "BRUSHES"

"brush"

LET THE CHILDREN PAINT WITH OBJECTS OTHER THAN BRUSHES

Bingo blotters
Castors
Combs
Corn cobs
Cotton swabs
Deodorant bottles
Dowels
Feathers
Foam rubber
Fly swatters
Golf balls
Hair rollers
Jar lids
Kitchen utensils
Marbles
Pine branches
Plastic baskets
Plastic puzzle pieces
Rolling pins
Small feather dusters
Spools
Sponges
Stamps and paint pads
Strings
Toy vehicles
Yarn

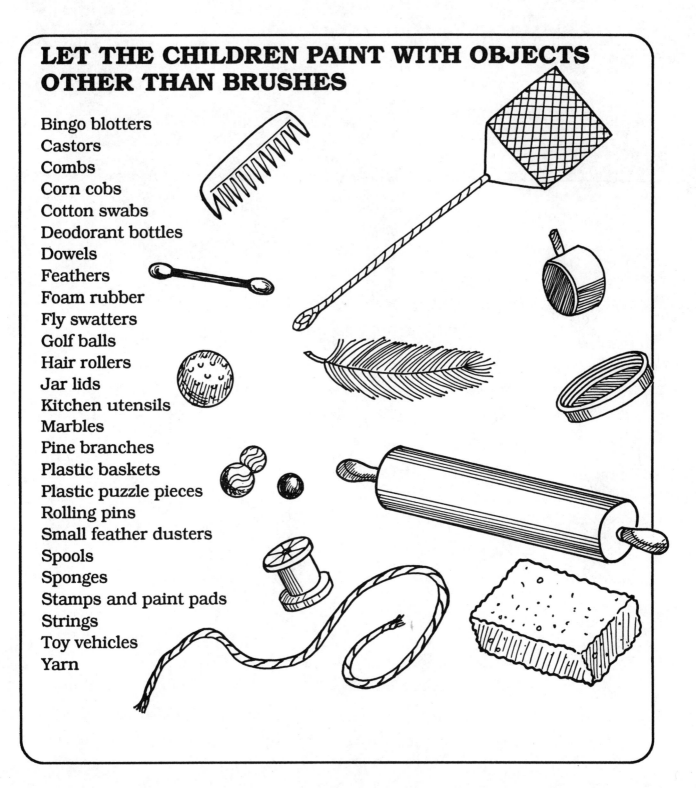

Using Fingerpaints

PETROLEUM JELLY FINGERPAINTING

spoon
~
smear

SIZE OF GROUP: Individual children or small group
DO THE ACTIVITY: At the Art Table

SUPPLIES AND MATERIALS

Petroleum jelly
Several large pieces of bubble pack
Tablespoon

PREPARATION

None

ACTIVITY

Tape the large pieces of bubble pack to the art table. Have the children put on smocks and push up their sleeves.

"Spoon" a small scoop of petroleum jelly on the bubble pack in front of each child as he comes to the art table. Let him *"smear"* it on the bubble pack as he chooses. When he's finished smearing it around, have him rub his hands together like hand lotion. If he has too much petroleum jelly left on his hands, let him wipe them with a paper towel.

EXTENSION

FINGERPAINT AND TALK

Sit down and fingerpaint with the children.
This not only makes them feel more comfortable,
but makes conversation easier.
> *"I like going up and down the bumps.
> (Child's name), you're
> going up and down too."*
> *"Look, I'm fingerpainting with the
> palm of my hand."*

VARIATIONS:

HAND LOTION FINGERPAINTING

Instead of petroleum jelly, use:
☛ Liquid hand lotion on aluminum foil wallpaper
☛ Cold cream on oilcloth

SOAP FINGERPAINTING

SIZE OF GROUP: Individual children or pairs
DO THE ACTIVITY: At the Art Table

SUPPLIES AND MATERIALS

Liquid dish soap
Pump-type bottles
Rubber bath mats with
   suction-cup bottoms
Paper towels

PREPARATION

☛ Pour small amounts
of dish soap into
pump bottles.

ACTIVITY

Tape the rubber mats upside-down on the art table, so the suctioned bottoms are face-up. Have the children push up their sleeves.

Let each child *"pump"* a puddle of dish soap on the mat and then begin to *"smear"* it all around. Encourage children to go slowly and feel the little bumps in their mats. *"What do the bumps feel like?"* Now go fast. *"How do your fingers feel?"*

Let each child continue fingerpainting for as long as he would like. If he needs more soap, let him *"pump"* what he needs. After he has finished, give him a paper towel to wipe off the mat so that it is ready for the next child.

HINT: Refill the pump bottles with
soap as needed. It is better to
continually refill the bottles than
to put too much in each one.

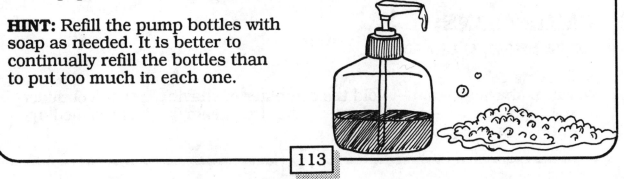

SHAVING CREAM FINGERPAINTING

SIZE OF GROUP: Small or large group of children
DO THE ACTIVITY: At the Art Table

SUPPLIES AND MATERIALS

Regular or menthol shaving cream
Several large pieces of clear plexiglass
Tempera paint
Squeeze bottles, such as for ketchup
   and mustard

PREPARATION

☛ Pour the tempera paint
   into squeeze bottles.

ACTIVITY

Make several large loops of masking tape and put them on the backside of
the plexiglass. Secure the plexiglass to the table. Have the children put on
smocks and push up their sleeves. (This can be a messy activity.)

"Spray" a hill of shaving cream in front of each child. Let her *"smear"* it
around the plexiglass for as long as she would like. Spray more shaving
cream if she needs it.

After she has fingerpainted for awhile, ask her if she would like to add a
little color to her shaving cream. If she says *"yes,"* squeeze just a little
liquid tempera paint onto the plexiglass and then encourage her to mix the
paint into the shaving cream.

HINT: Spray the plexiglass with a little water before doing the activity. A
wet surface is slippery and makes it easier to fingerpaint.

VARIATIONS:

MORE SHAVING CREAM

☛ Shaving gel
☛ Warm shaving cream -- Hold the container of shaving cream/gel under
   hot tap water for several minutes. After the cream/gel has warmed up,
   spray it on the plexiglass.

CINNAMON GLUE FINGERPAINTING

SIZE OF GROUP: Small group
DO THE ACTIVITY: At the Art Table

SUPPLIES AND MATERIALS

Flour
Water
Small pitchers
Cinnamon
Large cookie sheets
Poster putty

PREPARATION

☛ *"Mix"* a large batch of thick FLOUR AND WATER PASTE. (See basic recipe on page 152.) Add more flour to make it thick enough for fingerpaint.) Cover it until ready to use.

☛ Just before the activity pour the PASTE into small pitchers.

ACTIVITY

Put poster putty on the backsides of the cookie sheets to secure them to the art table. Have the children put on smocks and push their sleeves up high.

Pour a puddle of paste on a cookie sheet in front of each child when he wants to fingerpaint. (Encourage several children to paint on the same tray.) As the children are *"smearing"* the paste, ask each of them if they would like you to sprinkle a little cinnamon on their fingerpaint. If a child says *"yes,"* sprinkle some in the middle of his paste and let him continue to fingerpaint. Continue sprinkling cinnamon for each child who wants it.

VARIATIONS
A LITTLE COLOR
Have dry tempera paint in salt shakers. As the children are fingerpainting ask them if they would like you to add a little color to their paste. Shake colors as the children want.

FINGERPAINT AND PRINT

SIZE OF GROUP: Small group
DO THE ACTIVITY: At the Art Table

SUPPLIES AND MATERIALS

Different colors of pre-mixed commercial fingerpaint
Easel paper

PREPARATION

None

ACTIVITY

Have the children put on smocks and push up their sleeves.

When each child wants to fingerpaint, scoop some fingerpaint in front of
him and let him *"smear"* it around on the table for as long as he would like.
Give him more fingerpaint when he wants it.

MAKE THE PRINTS

After each child has finished, make a
"print" of her fingerpainting. Lay a
new piece of paper over her
painting, and then help her
firmly rub her hand over
the top of the paper.
Carefully lift the
paper up, look
at it, and
set it on
a shelf
to dry.

PASTE FINGERPAINTING

scoop ~ smear

SIZE OF GROUP: Small group
DO THE ACTIVITY: At the Art Table

SUPPLIES AND MATERIALS

White paste
Scoop
Spray bottle
Several large pieces of pegboard
Sponges

PREPARATION

☛ Fill the spray bottles with water.

☛ Fill a dish tub with a little water. Add several sponges.

ACTIVITY

Tape the pegboard to the table. Have the children put on their smocks and push up their sleeves.

"Scoop" a mound of paste on the pegboard in front of each child as she comes to fingerpaint. Let her *"smear"* the paste for as long as she would like. Add more paste if she needs it.

When each child is finished fingerpainting, have him wipe off his pegboard with a damp sponge. (Easy way to prevent the build-up of dried paste.)

HINT: If the paste gets dry as the children are fingerpainting, spray the children's hands or the paste with a little water.

VARIATIONS:
FROST THE BIRTHDAY CAKE
Have small spatulas or tongue depressors and several sheet or round cake pans. Put the pans upside down on the table. Let the children pretend to *"frost"* the cakes as they smear paste over the pans with the spatulas/ tongue depressors. As they *"frost"* their cakes, sing *Happy Birthday*.

MUD FINGERPAINTING

SIZE OF GROUP: Small or large group
DO THE ACTIVITY: Outside

SUPPLIES AND MATERIALS

Dirt
Water
Dish soap
Dish tub
Large piece of artificial turf
   or several large door mats
Containers with lids

PREPARATION

☞ Mix the Mud Fingerpaint:

1. Scoop the dirt into
   the dish tub.

2. Slowly add water, mixing
   the entire time.

3. After it is the right consistency,
   mix in a little dish soap. This will
   make the mud glossy and slippery.

4. Scoop it into container and cover.

ACTIVITY

Lay the artificial turf/mats in a quiet place within the outdoor play area,
preferably near a water source. Have the children put on smocks and push
up their sleeves.

When each child wants to MUD FINGERPAINT, scoop a mound of mud in
front of him on the artificial grass. Let him *"smear"* the mud on the grass for
as long as he wants. Give him more as he needs it.

After he's finished, help him wash his hands. Just before going inside, hose
off the mats and let them dry.

PUMPKIN GOO FINGERPAINTING

SIZE OF GROUP: Small or large group
DO THE ACTIVITY: In the Water Table

SUPPLIES AND MATERIALS

Several large pumpkins
Large plastic trays

PREPARATION

☛ Cut the tops off the pumpkins
and then clean them out with
the children. Put the *"insides"*
of the pumpkins (pumpkin goo)
in a large bowl. Set the pumpkins
on a shelf for the children to see.

ACTIVITY

Put several plastic trays in the water
table. Have the children put on their
smocks. *"Scoop"* big mounds of
pumpkin goo on the trays. Let
the children *"smear"* the goo around.

EXTENSION

PUMPKIN SEED DROP
Separate the Pumpkin Seeds:
    1. Have a brownie pan handy when you are cleaning your pumpkin/s.
       Let the children put the pumpkin seeds in the pan.
    2. Wash and dry the seeds and then put them back in the pan.
    3. Get two margarine tubs with tops. Cut several large holes in the tops
       and put them back on the tubs.

Play Pumpkin Seed Drop:
    1. Let the children drop the
       seeds into the holes.
    2. After they have dropped all
       the seeds, dump them back into the
       brownie pan and play PUMPKIN SEED DROP again and again.

TEXTURED FINGERPAINTING

SIZE OF GROUP: Small group
DO THIS ACTIVITY: At the Art Table

SUPPLIES AND MATERIALS

Home made or pre-mixed
    commercial fingerpaint
Different textures, such as:

Rice
Cornmeal
Crushed egg shells
Corn starch
Confetti

Birdseed
Sawdust
Soap powder

PREPARATION

☛ Choose different
textures and mix
them with different
colors of fingerpaint.
Put each textured
paint in a covered
container.

ACTIVITY

Put several trays on the table. Put on smocks and push up their sleeves.

When each child wants to fingerpaint, scoop some textured paint on a tray.
Let him *"smear"* the paint for as long as he would like. Give him more if he
wants.

When several children are fingerpainting, sit with them and fingerpaint. As
you and the children are painting, talk about what everyone is doing and
how it feels. You might say:

☛ *"I'm using my fingertips to smear my paint in circles. (Child's name),
you're using your whole hand."*
☛ *"(Child's name) put some paint on your fingers. How does it feel?"*
☛ *"I'm going to smear my paint very slowly and try to feel the 'sand' in the
paint. Maybe you will want to do it with me."*

SMELLY FINGERPAINTING

SIZE OF GROUP: Small group
DO THE ACTIVITY: At the Art Table

SUPPLIES AND MATERIALS

Home made or pre-mixed commercial fingerpaint
Plastic carpet protector
Several shaker bottles with very small holes
Different scents, such as:
> Extracts
>> Vanilla
>> Peppermint
>> Spearmint
>> Wintergreen
>
> Spices
>> Cinnamon
>> Clove
>> Pumpkin
>
> Lemon juice
> Unsweetened, powdered drink mixes
> Unsweetened gelatins
> Baby powder/talcum powder

PREPARATION

☛ Choose one scent each time you do this activity. Pour that liquid or dry scent into shaker bottles.

ACTIVITY

Tape the carpet protector to the table. Have the children put on smocks and push up their sleeves.

When each child wants to fingerpaint, scoop some paint on the carpet protector in front of him. Let him *"smear"* the paint for a little while. Then ask him, *"Would you like me to shake some good smelling powder/liquid on your paint?"* If he says, *"Yes,"* shake a little on his paint. Let him continue to fingerpaint, mixing in the *"smell"* as he does. Talk about the smell. Ask him if he likes it. Does he want more fingerpaint? More smell?

BUMPY FINGERPAINTING

smear ~ feel

SIZE OF GROUP: Small or large group
DO THE ACTIVITY: Outside

SUPPLIES AND MATERIALS

Home made or pre-mixed commercial fingerpaint
Fingerpaint paper
Wide tape

PREPARATION

☞ Roll up sheets of fingerpaint paper to carry outside.

ACTIVITY

Bring the smocks, paper, and fingerpaint outside.

When each child wants to fingerpaint, tape a piece of paper to the concrete or sidewalk for her. Scoop a mound of fingerpaint on the paper and let her *"smear"* it around for as long as she would like. Give the children more paint as they need it.

Ask the children if they can *"feel"* the cement under the paper as they paint. What does it feel like? Can they feel any bumps? What could they be?

After each child finishes, hang her painting on the fence to dry.

WINDOW FINGERPAINTING

SIZE OF GROUP: Individual or small group
DO THE ACTIVITY: On low windows

SUPPLIES AND MATERIALS

Pre-mixed, commercial fingerpaint
Liquid dish soap
Small sponges
Low stools

PREPARATION

☛ Mix a little dish soap with the
fingerpaint. (This will make
clean-up much easier.)

☛ Put the paint in small tubs with covers.

☛ Tape newspaper to the window sills,
walls around the windows, and
floor under the window.

ACTIVITY

Set the stools near the low windows. Put a sponge in each tub of
fingerpaint. Put on smocks and push up sleeves as high as possible.

Put scoops of fingerpaint on the sponges. Wipe the paint near the bottom of
each window. Let the children *"smear"* it all over the window as high as they
can reach. Some children may want to make designs in the paint with their
fingers or knuckles. Give the children more or different colors of paint as
they need it.

Leave the decorated windows for everyone to see. After an appropriate
length of time, clean them with damp paper towels or sponges.

VARIATION

MORE WINDOW DECORATING
Instead of using soapy fingerpaint, use shaving cream.

SOAP POWDER FINGERPAINT RECIPE

SUPPLIES AND MATERIALS

3 cups of soap powder
1 cup liquid starch
1 cup cold water
Large mixing bowl
Whisk
Food coloring

MAKE THE FINGERPAINT

1. Pour the soap powder into a large bowl.

2. Mix in the starch.

3. Add the cold water and whip until thoroughly mixed.

VARIATION

Add food coloring to the water and whip it into the mixture.

STORE THE FINGERPAINT

Put the fingerpaint in a covered container. Use it within several days, as it dries quickly.

SOAP POWDER FINGERPAINTING

SIZE OF GROUP: Individuals or small groups
DO THE ACTIVITY: At Any Table

SUPPLIES AND MATERIALS

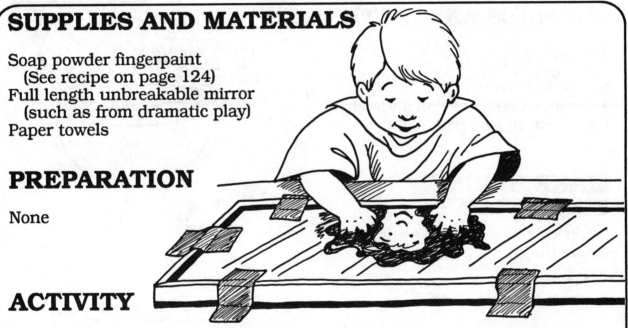

Soap powder fingerpaint
   (See recipe on page 124)
Full length unbreakable mirror
   (such as from dramatic play)
Paper towels

PREPARATION

None

ACTIVITY

Lay the mirror flat on the table, near an edge. Tape it down so that it does not move. Have the children put on their smocks.

When a child wants to SOAP POWDER FINGERPAINT, scoop a mound of paint on the mirror in front of him. Let him *"smear"* it around as long as he wants. Give the children more paint as they need it. When each child finishes fingerpainting, have him *"wipe-off"* the mirror with a paper towel. Now it is ready for another painter.

HINTS:
☛ If the soap powder paint gets too dry, spray it with water or let the children dip their fingers in a bowl of water.

☛ Repeat this activity several days in a row. Children spend a lot of time with this activity. They like to play *"peek-a-boo"* with themselves in the mirror as they paint.

STICKY FINGERPAINT RECIPE

SUPPLIES AND MATERIALS

1 cup flour
1 cup cold water
3 cups hot water
1T alum (preservative on spice shelf)
Food coloring/tempera paint

MAKE STICKY FINGERPAINT

(Make this fingerpaint
before the children arrive.)

1. Mix the flour and 1 cup of cold
   water in a large bowl.

2. Carefully pour the boiling water
   into the bowl. Stir the ingredients
   until they are mixed.

3. Pour the mixture into a large pan
   and cook until it boils. Stir continually.

4. Add the alum and coloring. Stir until
   you have colored fingerpaint.

5. Repeat the process for each color.

STORE THE FINGERPAINT

Spoon the STICKY FINGERPAINT into a
covered container. Store it in
the refrigerator.

STICKY FINGERPAINTING

SIZE OF GROUP: Small group
DO THE ACTIVITY: At the Art Table

SUPPLIES AND MATERIALS

Sticky fingerpaint (See recipe page 126)
Oilcloth
Squeeze bottles, such as for ketchup

PREPARATION

☛ Pour the fingerpaint into several
squeeze bottles.

ACTIVITY

Tape the oilcloth to the art table. Put on smocks and push up sleeves.

When children want to fingerpaint, *"squeeze"* a big puddle of STICKY
FINGERPAINT in front of them on the oilcloth. Let them *"smear"* the paint
around for as long as they would like. Give them more as they need it.

VARIATION

PAINT ON PAPER
This is a very nice fingerpaint to use on paper, because it does not curl
or wrinkle when the paint dries. Simply tape fingerpaint paper to the art
table and let the children paint. When it dries, let the children take their
paintings home.

EASY-MIX FINGERPAINT RECIPE

SUPPLIES AND MATERIALS

2 cups liquid starch
Soap powder
Baby powder/talcum powder
Tempera paint

MAKE EASY-MIX FINGERPAINT

1. Pour the liquid starch in a large bowl.

2. Stir in the soap powder and baby powder until you have a smooth fingerpaint consistency.

3. Pour a little tempera paint into the mixture and stir until it is thoroughly mixed. Add more paint it necessary.

4. Repeat the process for different colors of fingerpaint.

STORE THE FINGERPAINT

Pour the EASY-MIX FINGERPAINT in a covered container. Store it in the refrigerator.

EASY-MIX FINGERPAINTING

SIZE OF GROUP: Small group
DO THE ACTIVITY: At the Art Table

SUPPLIES AND MATERIALS

Easy-mix fingerpaint (See recipe page 128.)
Squeeze bottles, such as ketchup/mustard
Butcher paper
Different types of collage paper

PREPARATION

☛ Pour the fingerpaint into squeeze bottles.

☛ Cut the butcher paper to fit the art table.

☛ Tear/cut the collage
paper into small pieces.
(Children can do this the
day before fingerpainting.)

collage paper

ACTIVITY

Tape the butcher paper to the art table. Have the children put on smocks.

Squeeze large puddles of EASY-MIX FINGERPAINT on the butcher paper.
Let the children *"smear"* it around for as long as they would like. Add more
fingerpaint as the children need it.

After the children have fingerpainted, bring out the box of collage paper
pieces. Let the children *"stick"* the different pieces of paper all over the
butcher paper. After the paint has dried, hang the mural for everyone to
see.

Our Fingerpaint Collage

EASIEST-MIX FINGERPAINT

smear ~ color

SIZE OF GROUP: Small or large group
DO THE ACTIVITY: At the Art Table

SUPPLIES AND MATERIALS

Liquid laundry starch
Powdered tempera paint
Squeeze bottles such as ketchup/mustard
Unbreakable salt shakers
Large, textured surface, such as:

    Plastic carpet protector   Piece of formica
    Piece of panelling   Cookie sheets
    Rubber shower mats   Sheet cake pans
    Oil cloth   Plastic placemats
        Bubble pack

PREPARATION

☛ Pour the liquid starch into squeeze bottles.

☛ Pour different colors of dry tempera paint into salt shakers.

ACTIVITY

Tape the textured surface to the art table. Have the children put on their smocks and push up their sleeves.

When a child wants to fingerpaint, squeeze a puddle of starch on the textured surface in front of him. Let him *"smear"* the starch around for a little while and then ask him, *"Would you like me to shake red, blue or yellow powder on your fingerpaint?"* Shake the color he names, and let him mix it into the starch.

HINTS
☛ Have paper towels handy for the children to wipe their hands on.

☛ The first several times the children fingerpaint, you might want them to do it right on the art table, rather than on a textured surface.

MORE EASIEST-MIX FINGERPAINTING:
MEDIA MIXER
Use the commercial product, Media Mixer® as the basis of your fingerpaint, instead of liquid starch. Simply spoon a mound of it in front of a child. Let him smear it around and then sprinkle the color on it for him to mix.

PAINT DRIZZLE FINGERPAINTING

SIZE OF GROUP: Small group
DO THE ACTIVITY: At the Art Table

SUPPLIES AND MATERIALS

Tempera paint
Butcher paper
Squeeze bottles
Wide, stubby brushes

PREPARATION

☛ Pour each color of tempera paint into a squeeze bottle.

☛ Cut butcher paper the size of your art table.

ACTIVITY

Tape butcher paper to the art table. Have the children put on smocks and push up their sleeves.

"Drizzle" one or more colors of paint over a portion of the butcher paper. Let the children *"smear"* the drizzled paint. Drizzle more as they need it. Continue drizzling and smearing, until the whole paper is filled with lots of color.

HINT: You may want to use colors which blend into other colors, such as red and yellow blend into orange.

Using Glues and Pastes

COLORED GLUE RECIPE

mix ~ save

SUPPLIES AND MATERIALS

White glue
Food coloring
Popsicle sticks
Margarine tubs with tops

MAKE THE COLORED GLUE

1. Pour a little white glue into a margarine tub.

2. Slowly, so the children can see what is happening, squeeze one color of food coloring on top of the glue.

3. Put a popsicle stick in the bowl and let the children take turns stirring the glue. Keep stirring until the food coloring is totally mixed with the glue.

4. Repeat the mixing activity to make different colors.

EXTENSION

After children have had lots of one-color mixing experiences, use two colors of food coloring and let the children see what happens as they stir the colors into the glue.

STORE THE GLUE

Cover each margarine tub after you have colored the glue. Keep the glue covered when it is not being used.

GLUE DRIZZLE

SIZE OF GROUP: Individual children
DO THE ACTIVITY: Anyplace in the room

SUPPLIES AND MATERIALS

Colored glue (See recipe on page 134.)
Small squeeze bottles, such as tiny glue bottles
Heavy paper such as paper bags or
    cereal box cardboard
Several dish tubs

PREPARATION

☛ Pour colored glue into small squeeze bottles.

☛ Cut paper to fit in the dish tubs.

ACTIVITY

Set the dish tubs, paper, and glue on a table. Have the children put on smocks before they begin to use the glue.

Let each child put a piece of paper in a tub and then *"drizzle"* glue all over his paper. After he's finished, help him take the paper out and set it in a safe place to dry.

After the glue has dried, hang the children's COLORED GLUE DRIZZLES on a wall or bulletin board.

VARIATIONS

☛ Let children *"drizzle"* white glue on dark construction paper.

☛ Let children *"drizzle"* more than one color of glue.

MAGAZINE TEARING

SIZE OF GROUP: Any size group
DO THE ACTIVITY: On a Table

SUPPLIES AND MATERIALS

Magazines with lots of pictures
Shallow box

PREPARATION

☛ Tear out magazine pages with pictures on them.

ACTIVITY

Put several magazine pages and a shallow box on the table.

Let the children *"look"* at the magazine pages, *"tear out"* pictures they like, and place them in the box. Keep putting more pages on the table as the children tear-up the ones that are already there.

"Save" the magazine pictures for MAGAZINE COLLAGE the next day.

HINT: Avoid putting too many pages on the table at one time.

MAGAZINE COLLAGE

SIZE OF GROUP: Small group
DO THE ACTIVITY: At the Art Table

SUPPLIES AND MATERIALS

Magazine pictures which children
   have previously torn (See page 136.)
Butcher paper
Glue
Cotton swabs

PREPARATION

☛ Pour a little glue into
   small containers.

☛ Cut butcher paper to
   fit on the art table.

ACTIVITY

Tape the butcher paper to the table.
Set some of the magazine pictures on it.
Have the children put on smocks and push
up their sleeves before they begin gluing.

Give the children containers of glue. Have them *"brush"* glue on the paper
with the cotton swabs and then *"stick"* the pictures on the glue.

HINTS:

☛ Remember that brushing the glue is the *"most fun"* part of this activity
   and children will spend most of their time doing it.

☛ Set a minimal amount of pictures on the table. Keep adding more as the
   children need them.

☛ Replace the cotton swabs when they get *"stringy"* and difficult to use.

PAPER TEARING

SIZE OF GROUP: Any size
DO THE ACTIVITY: In the Water Table

SUPPLIES AND MATERIALS

One type of paper
Shallow box

PREPARATION

☛ Tear or cut the paper into appropriate size pieces for your children to tear.

ACTIVITY

Put a few sheets of paper and the box in the water table. Let the children *"tear"* the paper into smaller pieces and put them in the box. Add more paper as the children need it.

"Save" the paper to use for PAPER GLUING the next day.

PAPER GLUING

SIZE OF GROUP: Small group
DO THE ACTIVITY: In the Water Table

SUPPLIES AND MATERIALS

Small pieces of paper which the
   children have previously torn
   (See page 138.)
Brown craft paper
Glue
Small squeeze bottles, such
   as glue bottles

PREPARATION

☛ Pour a little glue into
   squeeze bottles.

☛ Cut the brown paper to fit
   in the water table.

ACTIVITY

Tape the brown paper to fit in the water table. Set the bottles of glue and
some pieces of paper next to the table. Remind the children to put on
smocks and push up their sleeves before they glue.

Let the children *"drizzle"* some glue on the brown paper and then *"stick"*
small pieces of paper on their drizzle lines. Let each child continue drizzling
and sticking for as long as he would like.

VARIATION

MORE PAPER GLUING
Do this activity often, using different types of paper.

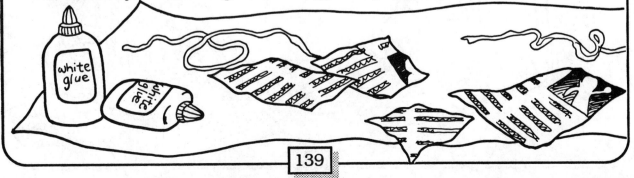

GLUE PAINTING

SIZE OF GROUP: Individual or small group
DO THE ACTIVITY: At the Art Table

SUPPLIES AND MATERIALS

White glue
Food coloring
Any type of paper
Cotton swabs

PREPARATION

☛ Color the glue by mixing it with
  different colors of food coloring.
  Pour a little of each color into a
  small container with a lid.

ACTIVITY

Remind the children to put on their smocks.

When a child wants to do this activity, give her paper, a container of colored
glue, and a cotton swab. Let her *"spread and smear"* glue on her paper.
After she has finished painting with one color, ask her if she'd like another
one. Exchange the first color for the second one and let her continue.

HINT: Be sure to have lots of cotton swabs, so that you can give the
children new ones when the cotton gets too *"stringy"* or *"gooey."*

COTTON BALL GLUING

SIZE OF GROUP: Small group
DO THE ACTIVITY: At the Art Table

SUPPLIES AND MATERIALS

Busing tubs or large shallow trays such as brownie pans
Colored cottons balls (Commercial or homemade)
Glue
Margarine tubs
Manilla paper
Stubby paint brushes

PREPARATION

☛ Pour a little glue into several margarine tubs.

☛ Color the Cotton Balls. To color each bunch:
   1. Pour a very small amount of powdered tempera paint into a small bag.
   2. Put 10-15 balls in the bag and shake.

ACTIVITY

Put several large trays on the table. Before each child begins gluing, remind her to put on a smock and push up her sleeves.

Have the children put paper on one of the trays. (Encourage two or three children to share a tray.) Let them use paint brushes to *"spread"* glue on their paper. After they have spread as much glue as they would like, hand them several cotton balls at a time to *"stick"* on their paper. If they want they can spread more glue and then add more cotton balls. Let each child continue for as long as she would like.

HINTS:
☛ You may have to *"spread"* the glue on the paper for younger children since a two-step gluing activity is oftentimes too involved.

☛ Cleaning Tip: After the children have finished, soak the brushes in hot water as soon as possible.

COMIC PAPER WADDING

SIZE OF GROUP: Small group
DO THE ACTIVITY: In the Water Table

SUPPLIES AND MATERIALS

Colored comic sections of your local newspaper
Shoe box

PREPARATION

☛ Cut/tear the comic pages
into 4"-6"squares.

ACTIVITY

Set some of the paper squares in
the water table. Put the shoe box in the middle.

Let the children *"wad"* the squares into balls and put them in the shoe box.
Keep adding more paper squares as the children need them. *"Save"* the
wads to use for COMIC WAD GLUING.

VARIATIONS
OTHER PAPERS

Do this activity often, using different types of paper:
    ☛ Colored advertising sections of the newspaper
    ☛ Tissue paper (Cut/tear 6"-8" squares instead of 4"-6" ones.)
    ☛ Aluminum foil   ☛ Paper bags   ☛ Foil-type wallpaper

COMIC WAD GLUING

spread
~
stick

SIZE OF GROUP: Any size group
DO THE ACTIVITY: In the Water Table

SUPPLIES AND MATERIALS

Comic paper wads
Egg cartons
Glue
Cotton swabs
Small containers

PREPARATION

☛ Pour a little glue into small containers.

☛ Cut the lids off the egg cartons. Save them for another activity.

ACTIVITY

Put several egg cartons and containers of glue in the water table. Have cotton swabs available. Remind the children to put on smocks.

Let the children *"spread"* as much glue in the egg carton cups as they want. After each child has finished gluing, give him several wads to *"stick"* on the glue. Keep giving him more wads until he has stuck as many as he wants.

☛ Put the cartons on a shelf to dry.

☛ Add more egg cartons as needed.

☛ Hang the colorful cartons from the ceiling.

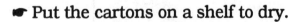

TONGUE DEPRESSOR PASTING

spread ~ smear

SIZE OF GROUP: Individual children
DO THE ACTIVITY: At the Art Table

SUPPLIES AND MATERIALS

Corrugated paper (see "hint" below)
Paste
Tongue depressors

PREPARATION

☞ Cut large piece/s of
corrugated paper into
individual pieces.

ACTIVITY

Remind each child to put on his smock and push up his sleeves.

When a child wants to paste, tape a piece of corrugated paper to the table
for him. Spoon a large scoop of paste onto his paper. Let him *"spread and
smear"* the paste all around the paper with a tongue depressor. Give him
more scoops of paste as he wants them.

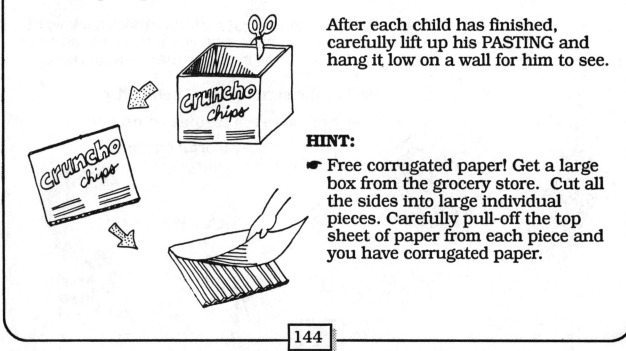

After each child has finished,
carefully lift up his PASTING and
hang it low on a wall for him to see.

HINT:

☞ Free corrugated paper! Get a large
box from the grocery store. Cut all
the sides into large individual
pieces. Carefully pull-off the top
sheet of paper from each piece and
you have corrugated paper.

GREETING CARD GLUING

spread ~ stick

SIZE OF GROUP: Individual children
DO THE ACTIVITY: At the Art Table

SUPPLIES AND MATERIALS

Small paint brushes
Pizza boards
Small squeeze bottles,
    such as glue bottles
Greeting cards
Food coloring
White glue

PREPARATION

☛ Mix different food colorings with white glue. Pour a little of each color into small squeeze bottles.

☛ Cut the fronts off greeting cards.

ACTIVITY

Remind each child to put on her smock and push up her sleeves before beginning to glue.

Tape each child's pizza wheel to the table and drizzle a little glue on it. Let her *"spread"* the glue around with her brush. Ask her if she would like more glue. Drizzle more if she wants and let her continue to spread it on the pizza wheel. After she has spread as much glue as she wants, let her choose greeting cards to *"stick"* on her glue.

Punch a hole in the top of each wheel and loop a piece of yarn through it for a hanger. Let the children take them home to decorate their bedroom doors or front doors of their homes.

HINT: Cleaning Tip -- Put the brushes in hot water as soon as possible.

COLORED GLUE DRIZZLE

SIZE OF GROUP: Individual children
DO THE ACTIVITY: At the Art Table

SUPPLIES AND MATERIALS

White glue
Food coloring
Small squeeze bottles,
  such as glue bottles
Aluminum foil

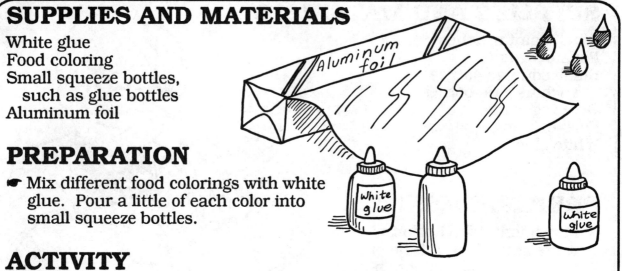

PREPARATION

☞ Mix different food colorings with white
  glue. Pour a little of each color into
  small squeeze bottles.

ACTIVITY

Remind each child to put on a smock before beginning.

Tape a piece of aluminum foil on the table for each child as he begins
COLORED GLUE DRIZZLING. Give him a bottle of colored glue and let him
"drizzle" as much as he'd like on his foil. After awhile ask him if he'd like
another color. If he does, exchange the bottle he has for the new color.

After he has finished, set the DRIZZLING to the side to dry. Depending on
how much glue he has drizzled, it may take several days to completely dry.

BOX GLUING

brush
~
stick

SIZE OF GROUP: Small group
DO THE ACTIVITY: In the Water Table

SUPPLIES AND MATERIALS

Large, sturdy cardboard box
White glue
Small paste brushes
Variety of textures, such as:
    Craft feathers
    Pieces of sandpaper
    Rubber bands
    Heavy yarn
    Large paper clips

PREPARATION

☛ Pour small amounts of glue into several small containers.

ACTIVITY

Put the large box in the water table. Remind the children to put on their smocks and push up their sleeves.

As each child wants to BOX GLUE give her a container of glue and a brush. Let her *"brush"* as much glue on the box as she wants. Then hand her several textures to *"stick"* on the glue. Let her continue to brush glue and stick textures to the box for as long as she would like.

HINT: Cleaning Tip -- Put the brushes in hot water as soon as possible.

FABRIC ON FABRIC

SIZE OF GROUP: Small or large group
DO THE ACTIVITY: At a Large Table

SUPPLIES AND MATERIALS

White glue
Small squeeze bottles,
   such as glue bottles
Large piece of fabric
   such as a bedsheet
   or old tablecloth
Variety of textured fabrics:
     Felt
     Corduroy
     Denim
     Leather
     Wide ribbons
     Heavy yarn

PREPARATION

☛ Pour a little white glue
   into small squeeze bottles.

☛ Cut the fabric into small,
   manageable pieces.

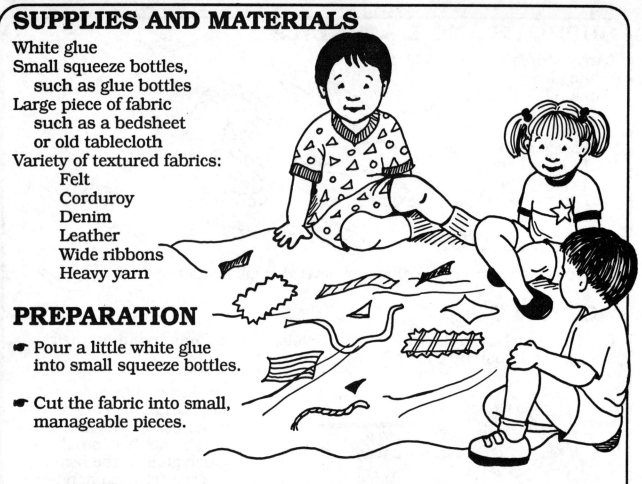

ACTIVITY

Tape the large piece of fabric to the table. Have the children wear smocks.

As each child wants to glue, give him several pieces of textured fabric. Have him put them on the large sheet anywhere he wants. Continue giving him several pieces at a time until he's *"arranged"* as many pieces of fabric as he wants. Then hand him a bottle of glue and let him *"drizzle"* glue over his fabric pieces.

Let the sheet dry overnight and then:
   ☛ Hang it in the room   ☛ Use it for a tablecloth
   ☛ Sit around it at group time.

NATURE GLUING

SIZE OF GROUP: Small group
DO THE ACTIVITY: At the Art Table

drizzle ~ stick

SUPPLIES AND MATERIALS

White glue
Small squeeze bottles, such as glue bottles
Brown mailing or butcher paper
Pieces of nature such as:

> Leaves
> Sticks
> Bark
> Grass
> Weeds
> Moss

PREPARATION

☛ Pour glue into small squeeze bottles.

☛ Collect things from nature.
(You could take a NATURE
WALK with the children
and let them pick up things
and put them in a box or bag.)

ACTIVITY

Tape a large piece of brown paper to the art table. Have the children wear smocks.

Let the children *"drizzle"* glue on the paper. After each child has finished drizzling, hand him several pieces of nature and let him *"stick"* them on the glue. Hand him several more pieces and let him continue.

HINT: As the children are making their NATURE GLUING, name and talk about the different things which were found outside .

CORK GLUING

brush ~ stick

SIZE OF GROUP: Individual children
DO THE ACTIVITY: At the Art Table

SUPPLIES AND MATERIALS

All sizes of corks
Large piece of flat, thick
   styrofoam (You could
   also use styrofoam
   plates.)
White glue
Food coloring
Cotton swabs

PREPARATION

☛ Break the styrofoam into
   small pieces.

☛ Mix different food
   colorings with white
   glue. Pour a little
   colored glue into
   small containers.

ACTIVITY

Set the supplies near the art table.
Have the children put on their smocks.

Give the children pieces of styrofoam and containers of glue with cotton
swabs. Let each child *"brush"* as much glue onto her styrofoam as she
wants. If she needs more or wants a different color glue, exchange the glue
containers. After she has brushed as much glue as she would like to, give
her several corks and let her *"stick"* them on the glue. Give her as many as
she wants. Let the CORK GLUINGS dry.

EXTENSION

SAILING ALONG
After the CORK GLUINGS have dried, let the children float them in the
water table or take them outside and play with them in a wading pool filled
with a little water.

ADHESIVE PAPER COLLAGE

SIZE OF GROUP: Small group
DO THE ACTIVITY: At Any Table

SUPPLIES AND MATERIALS

Clear adhesive paper
Variety of paper

PREPARATION

☛ Cut or tear the paper
into small pieces.

ACTIVITY

Tape the clear adhesive paper
upside-down on the table.

When a child wants to COLLAGE,
hand him several pieces of paper
and let him *"stick"* them on the
adhesive paper. Give each child
more paper as he needs it, and
let him continue to stick for as
long as he wants.

After the adhesive paper is full of colored paper, carefully pull it up and
hang it on your classroom door at the children's eye level. Tape another
piece of adhesive paper to the table and let the children *"stick"* some more.

HINT: The day before you do ADHESIVE PAPER COLLAGE, let the
children help you tear the paper into smaller pieces.

VARIATION
COLLECTING PAPER SCRAPS

Ask the teachers of older children to save all their paper scraps for the
younger children. Use these special scraps to do the activity. Hang the
finished COLLAGE in the hall with a message such as, *"Thank you for all
the paper scraps. The two year olds had lots of fun!"*

FLOUR-WATER GLUE RECIPE

SUPPLIES AND MATERIALS

1 cup flour
1 1/4 cups water
Large bowl
Mixing spoon
Measuring cup

MAKE THE GLUE

1. Pour flour into the large bowl.

2. Slowly add the water, stirring all of the time. Continue stirring until the glue is a creamy consistency.

3. Add more flour if the glue is too thin. Add more water if the glue is too thick.

STORE THE GLUE

Keep the glue in a covered container. Put it in the refrigerator if you are storing it overnight. Stir it again in the morning and let it get to room temperature.

CONFETTI GLUING

smear ~ stick

SIZE OF GROUP: Small or large group
DO THE ACTIVITY: At the Art Table

SUPPLIES AND MATERIALS

Large, corrugated box such as from the grocery store
Colored confetti or Easter grass
Flour-water glue (See recipe on page 152.)
Paint trim brush

PREPARATION

☞ Cut the corrugated box so that it is one large flat piece. Cut off the excess cardboard and save for another activity.

ACTIVITY

Tape the cardboard to the table. Remind the children to put on their smocks and push up their sleeves.

When children want to CONFETTI GLUE, put big scoops of flour-water glue in front of them on the cardboard and then let them *"smear"* it all around with their brushes. Give them more glue as they want it.

After each child has smeared as much glue as she wants, hand her a little confetti and let her *"stick"* it to the glue. Give her as much as she'd like.

Let the GLUING dry overnight. In the morning punch 5-6 holes across the top, tie heavy yarn through each hole, and hang the GLUING from your ceiling.

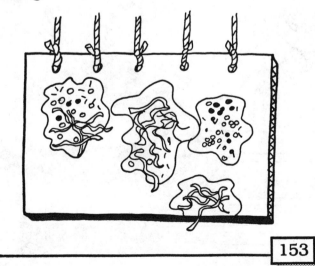

TISSUE PAPER TEARING

SIZE OF GROUP: Small group
DO THE ACTIVITY: In the Water Table

SUPPLIES AND MATERIALS

Different colors of tissue paper
Dish tub

PREPARATION

☛ Cut the large pieces of tissue paper into more manageable sizes.

ACTIVITY

Put one or two dish tubs in an empty water table. Give the children tissue paper. Let them *"tear"* the big pieces into smaller ones, and put them in a dish tub. After each child has finished tearing his big piece, give him another one if he wants. Let the children continue to tear and *"save"* for as long as they want.

HINT: If your children have not had much experience with tearing paper, cut the original sheets of tissue paper into strips rather than manageable-size pieces.

TISSUE PAPER GLUING

SIZE OF GROUP: Individual children
DO THE ACTIVITY: At the Art Table

SUPPLIES AND MATERIALS

Tissue paper
  which the children
  have previously torn
Liquid starch
Waxed paper
Squeeze bottle,
  such as
  a ketchup
  or mustard
  bottle

PREPARATION

☛ Pour liquid starch into squeeze bottles.

ACTIVITY

Have the children put on smocks and push up their shirt sleeves.

When a child wants to TISSUE PAPER GLUE, tape a piece of waxed paper to the art table in front of him. Let him squeeze some liquid starch onto his paper and then *"smear"* it around with his fingers for as long as he would like. Let him squeeze more starch if he wants and continue to smear.

After each child has smeared the starch for as long as he wants, give him several pieces of tissue paper to *"stick"* on the starch. Continue giving him tissue paper until he his finished.

Let the children's GLUINGS dry and then hang them in sunny windows. *"How do they look when the sun is shining on them?"*

PEANUT PIECES GLUING

SIZE OF GROUP: Individual children
DO THE ACTIVITY: At the Art Table

SUPPLIES AND MATERIALS

Paper plates
White glue
Small squeeze bottles, such as glue bottles
Dry tempera
Colored styrofoam peanuts

PREPARATION

☛ Make colored glue by stirring dry tempera paint into the white
glue. (You could use food coloring instead of dry tempera.)

☛ Pour a little colored glue into small squeeze bottles.

ACTIVITY

Remind the children to put on their smocks before doing the activity.

Let the children *"drizzle"* colored glue on their paper plates. They may want
to use more than one color glue. If so, exchange the color each child is
using for a new one.

After each child has drizzled enough glue, give him several peanuts to
"stick" on his glue lines. Keep giving each child several peanuts at a time,
until he has stuck as many as he wants.

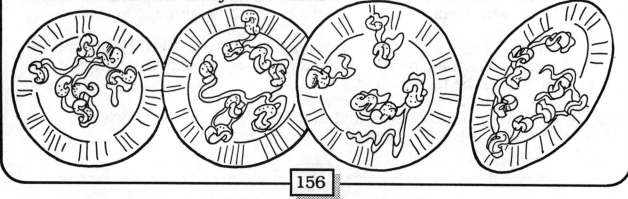

YARN GLUING

arrange
~
drizzle

SIZE OF GROUP: Individual children
DO THE ACTIVITY: At the Art Table

SUPPLIES AND MATERIALS

Waxed paper
White glue
Small squeeze bottles, such as
   glue bottles
Very heavy yarn
Box tops from gift or shoe boxes

PREPARATION

☞ Cut the yarn into short pieces (4" to 8").

☞ Pour a little white glue into small
   squeeze bottles.

ACTIVITY

Remind the children to put on smocks.

As each child wants to YARN GLUE, help her lay a piece of waxed paper in a box top. Give her several pieces of yarn and let her put them on the waxed paper. Hand her more yarn and let her continue *"arranging"* it.

After she has arranged as much yarn as she wants, give her a glue bottle and let her *"drizzle"* glue all over the yarn. Take the YARN GLUING out of the box top and let it dry. (Could take until the next day.)

VARIATIONS:

MORE GLUING
Instead of yarn, use:
   ☞ String
   ☞ Ribbon
   ☞ Twine
   ☞ Streamers

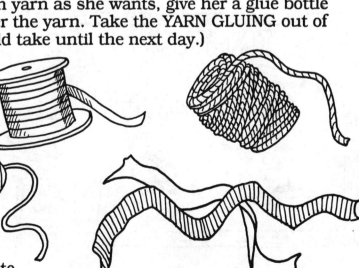

COLORED GLUE
Use colored glue instead of white.

DANDELION GLUING

SIZE OF GROUP: Individual or small group
DO THE ACTIVITY: At the Art Table

SUPPLIES AND MATERIALS

Box lids from shoe or gift boxes for all the children
White glue
Small squeeze bottles, such as glue bottles
Dandelions

PREPARATION

☛ Pour a little white glue into small squeeze bottles.

☛ Take the children on a DANDELION PICKING WALK. Let them pick dandelions and give them to you. Bring the giant bouquet inside.

ACTIVITY

Have the children put on their smocks.

Give each child a box top and a glue bottle. Let her *"drizzle"* as much glue on the box top as she wants and then *"stick"* dandelions all along the drizzle lines and in the glue puddles. Let them dry, and then hang them on the bulletin board for a Springtime Display.

HOLIDAY BAG GLUING

brush ~ stick

SIZE OF GROUP: Individual children
DO THE ACTIVITY: At the Art Table

SUPPLIES AND MATERIALS

Paper grocery bags
White glue
Small brushes
Holiday collage materials:
    Greeting cards
    Ribbons

PREPARATION

☞ Pour a little white glue into small containers. Add a brush to each container.
☞ Cut the collage materials into appropriate size pieces.

ACTIVITY

Remind the children to put on their smocks and push up their shirt sleeves.

Let the children brush glue on their bags. After there is enough glue, give the children holiday collage materials to *"stick"* on their bags. Keep giving each child materials until he has finished collaging his bag.

Let the bags dry overnight, and then let the children *"stick"* holiday materials on the other side of their bags the next day.

EXTENSION

AT HOME
Encourage families to use decorated bags during their holiday celebrations:
☞ To wrap a large gift.
☞ To store special gifts.
☞ To carry food or gifts to another person's home.

GLUE AND SHAKE SUPPLIES

SMALL-HOLED SHAKERS
Salt and pepper shakers
Sugar-cinnamon bears
Shakers with handles
Spice bottles with small holes

MATERIALS
Colored salt
Cornmeal
Dried coffee grounds

Sand
Talcum powder
Dried tempera paint
Flour
Poppy seeds
Dried tea grounds

MEDIUM-HOLED SHAKERS
Candy dot bottles
Spice bottles with large holes

MATERIALS
Bird seed
Colored rice

Plastic stir-sticks cut up into very
    tiny pieces
Dry dirt
Sequins
Dried and crushed egg shells
Kosher salt

LARGE-HOLED SHAKERS
Parmesan cheese containers

MATERIALS
Aquarium gravel
Dried field corn
Finely cut Easter grass/sparkle straw
Paper dots from print shops
Sawdust

Confetti circles
Grass seed
Oatmeal
Tiny noodles colored in food coloring
Popcorn kernels

GIANT-HOLED SHAKERS
Cylinder-shaped chip cans
Plastic handball cans
Peanut cans
Tennis ball cans
Cut appropriate size holes in the
lids. You may need to tape the lids
after you've added the material.

MATERIALS
Dried and crushed leaves

Narrow ribbons cut into quarter-
    inch pieces
Watermelon seeds
Pipe cleaners cut into quarter-inch
    pieces
Pumpkin seeds
Dried evergreen needles
Pebbles
Dried grass clippings

GLUE AND SHAKE FUN

apply
~
shake

SIZE OF GROUP: Individual or small group
DO THE ACTIVITY: In a Dish Tub for individual children.
In the Water Table for groups.

SUPPLIES AND MATERIALS

Any type of paper
Shakers
One or more of the materials listed on page 160
White glue

PREPARATION

☛ Pour small amounts of glue in the appropriate containers. Get
applicators if necessary.

☛ Put small amounts of one or several of the materials listed above
in the shaker bottles.

☛ Cut paper to fit in dish tubs or the water table.

ACTIVITY

Each time you set up a GLUE AND SHAKE activity, let the children brush
or drizzle the glue on the paper and then *"shake"* as much material as
they would like.

PEANUT BUTTER GLUING SNACK

(edible glue)
SIZE OF GROUP: Individual children
DO THE ACTIVITY: At a Table

SUPPLIES AND MATERIALS

Peanut butter
Crackers
Popsicle sticks or dull knives
Raisins
Small paper plates

PREPARATION

☛ Put the peanut butter in very small containers.

ACTIVITY

Wipe off and sanitize the table. Wash hands.

Give each child a small paper plate, a knife, a cracker, and a cup of peanut butter. Have him put the cracker on his plate and then *"spread"* the cracker with peanut butter. Let him do another one if he wants.

After he has finished spreading peanut butter, give him several raisins to *"stick"* on his cracker/s. Continue giving the children raisins until they have enough on their crackers.

CREAM CHEESE GLUING SNACK

(edible glue)
SIZE OF GROUP: Individual children
DO THE ACTIVITY: At a Table

SUPPLIES AND MATERIALS

Cream cheese
Apples
Popsicle sticks or dull knives
Cheerios®
Small paper plates

PREPARATION

☞ Put softened cream cheese in very small containers, such as individual mini cupcake liners. Add a knife/popsicle stick to each one.

ACTIVITY

Wipe off and sanitize the table you are going to use. Have the children wash their hands.

Let the children watch you cut the apples into small wedges. Put them in a bowl. Give each child a small paper plate, an apple wedge, and a cup of cream cheese. Have him put the apple on his plate and then *"spread"* the apple with cream cheese using the dull knife or popsicle stick. Let him spread cream cheese on another apple if he wants.

After he has finished spreading cream cheese, give him several Cheerios® to *"stick"* on his apple/s. Continue giving each child Cheerios® until each has enough on his apple wedge/s.

Eat the special apples for snack with a glass of milk.

VARIATION

GRAHAM CRACKER SNACK
Spread cream cheese on graham crackers and stick banana slices on top.

Using Chalks

WET CHALK

SIZE OF GROUP: Individual or small group
DO THE ACTIVITY: At the Art Table

SUPPLIES AND MATERIALS
Chalk
Water
Paper bags, especially
   brown grocery bags
Meat tray

PREPARATION

None

ACTIVITY

Pour a little water onto a
meat tray and set several
pieces of chalk in the water.
Have the children put on smocks.

Let the children use the wet chalk to *"draw"* on paper bags. Add more
chalk when necessary.

VARIATIONS

MORE WET CHALK
Instead of using water to wet
the chalk, use
  ☛ Liquid starch
  ☛ Buttermilk
  ☛ Sugar-water mixture --
    1/2 cup water to 1/6 cup sugar

CHALK ON WET PAPER

SIZE OF GROUP: Individual children
DO THE ACTIVITY: At the Art Table

SUPPLIES AND MATERIALS

Chalk
Individual pieces of paper
Dish tub
Cookie sheets (optional)

PREPARATION

☛ Fill a dish tub about half full of water.

One...
Two...

ACTIVITY

Tape cookie sheets to the table. Put the dish tub on the table. Have the children put on smocks.

When a child wants to use the chalk, *"dip"* a piece of paper in the water, count together *"1,2"* and then pull it out. Have the child set the paper on a cookie sheet or right on the art table. Hand her a piece of chalk and let her *"draw"* for as long as she would like.

HINT: Wet black paper stains tabletops and other surfaces.

CHALK ON CHALKBOARDS

draw ~ erase

SIZE OF GROUP: Individual children or small group
DO THE ACTIVITY: On the Floor or At a Table

SUPPLIES AND MATERIALS

Chalk
Chalkboard
4-5 erasers

PREPARATION

None

ACTIVITY

Tape a chalkboard to the table or floor. Put the erasers in a box next to the board. Have the children wear smocks.

Let the children *"draw"* on the chalkboard and *"erase"* their marks for as long as they would like.

HINT: Erasing the chalk marks is just as much fun and valuable as drawing them.

CHALK ON FABRIC

SIZE OF GROUP: Small or large group
DO THE ACTIVITY: At the Art Table

SUPPLIES AND MATERIALS

Chalk
Different types of fabric, such as:
    Bedsheets
    Towels
    Tablecloths
    Rug remnants

PREPARATION

None

ACTIVITY

Choose one type of fabric and tape it to the table. Have the children put on smocks.

Give the children chalk and let them *"smudge"* all over the fabric. When each child has smudged for as long as he wants, have him give you back the piece of chalk, and then *"smear"* his smudges by rubbing them with his fingers.

HINT: The children will probably want to smudge and smear several times. Simply give them back chalk each time. Remember, both activities are equally fun and appropriate.

CHALK ON LARGE TEXTURED PAPER

SIZE OF GROUP: Small or large group of children
DO THE ACTIVITY: At the Art Table

SUPPLIES AND MATERIALS

Chalk
Large sheets of textured paper, such as:
    Cardboard -- side of an appliance box
    Wallpaper
    Desk blotters
    Mailing paper
    Black/white newspaper
    Heavy-duty wrapping paper

PREPARATION

None

ACTIVITY

Choose one type of paper and tape it to the table. Have the children put on their smocks.

Give the children pieces of chalk and let them *"smudge and draw"* on the paper for as long as they would like. After children have colored for awhile, ask them if they would like a different color. If so, exchange pieces of chalk with them.

HINT: Do this activity often, using a different type of paper each time.

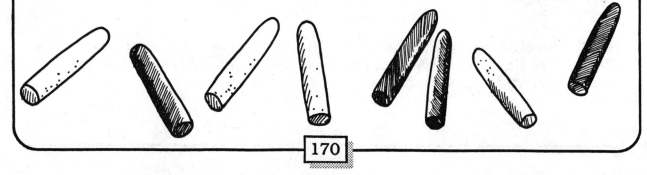

CHALK ON SMALL TEXTURED PAPER

smudge ~ draw

SIZE OF GROUP: Individual children
DO THE ACTIVITY: At the Art Table

SUPPLIES AND MATERIALS

Chalk
Small pieces of textured paper, such as:
  Sandpaper
  Paper grocery bags
  Corrugated cardboard
  Manilla paper
  Pizza boards
  Placemats
  Paper plates
  Lids of cardboard egg cartons

PREPARATION

None

ACTIVITY

Have the children put on their smocks.

When a child wants to use the chalk, tape his paper or cardboard to the table and give him a piece of chalk. Let him *"smudge and draw"* on it for as long as he would like. Switch colors with him if he wants.

CHALK ON DARK PAPER

SIZE OF GROUP: Small or large group
DO THE ACTIVITY: At the Art Table

SUPPLIES AND MATERIALS

White chalk
Dark butcher paper/studio
   photographer's
   background paper

PREPARATION

None

ACTIVITY

Tape the dark paper to the art table. Have the children put on smocks.

Give the children white chalk when they come to the table. Let them *"smudge and draw"* for as long as they want.

EXTENSION:

TALK A LITTLE
(Use this extension with children after they have had at least several opportunities to simply scribble with chalk.)

While they are smudging and drawing, sit at the table with them and encourage them to use their chalk in different ways, and then talk with them about how it looks. Encourage them to:

- ☛ Press hard with their chalk
- ☛ Press lightly with their chalk
- ☛ Draw giant circles, zigzags, and dots.

CHALK ON PEGBOARD

draw ~ erase

SIZE OF GROUP: Individuals or small group
DO THE ACTIVITY: At the Art Table

SUPPLIES AND MATERIALS

Chalk
Large piece of pegboard or
    several smaller pieces
Small sponges
Paper towels
Meat trays

PREPARATION

None

ACTIVITY

Tape the pegboard to the table. Pour a little water onto several meat trays. Dampen the sponges and set them on other meat trays. Place the sponges and paper towels near the activity, but not on the table.

Give the children chalk and let them *"draw"* on the pegboard for as long as they would like.

When each child is finished drawing, give her a sponge and have her *"erase"* her drawing. Then let her dry the board with a paper towel. Would she like to do it again?

HINTS:

☛ Have a spray bottle filled with water. If the sponges get too dry, simply spray them with a little water.

☛ Remember, the erasing process could take as long or longer than the drawing, and both are fun and valuable.

CHALK ON CARDBOARD

SIZE OF GROUP: Individuals or small group
DO THE ACTIVITY: At the Art Table

SUPPLIES AND MATERIALS

Chalk
Different types of cardboard, such as:
    Large cardboard trays from
      cafeterias and grocery produce
      departments
    Small appliance and grocery
      boxes
    Large cardboard tubes
      from newsprint, butcher paper,
      postoffice, wrapping paper, etc.
    Pizza boards
    Egg cartons

PREPARATION

None

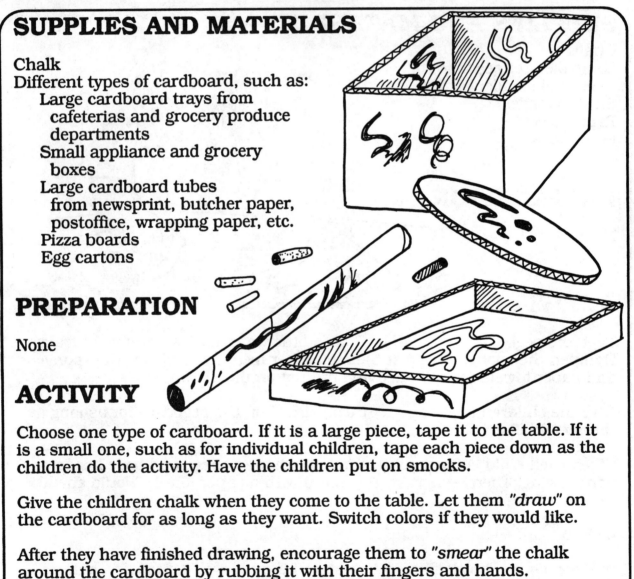

ACTIVITY

Choose one type of cardboard. If it is a large piece, tape it to the table. If it is a small one, such as for individual children, tape each piece down as the children do the activity. Have the children put on smocks.

Give the children chalk when they come to the table. Let them *"draw"* on the cardboard for as long as they want. Switch colors if they would like.

After they have finished drawing, encourage them to *"smear"* the chalk around the cardboard by rubbing it with their fingers and hands.

HINT: When the children are chalking appliance and grocery boxes, they like to color both the insides and outsides.

CHALK ON GIANT BOXES

SIZE OF GROUP: Small group
DO THE ACTIVITY: On the Floor, Next To a Wall

SUPPLIES AND MATERIALS

Jumbo chalk
Large boxes, such as from:
    Appliance stores
    Building supply stores
    Hardware stores
4-5 erasers

PREPARATION

None

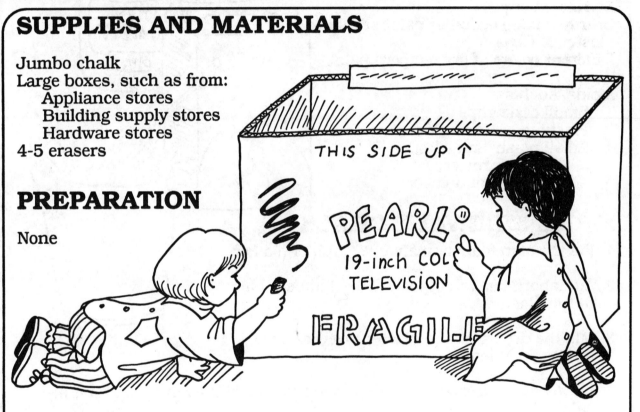

ACTIVITY

Tape the box to the wall, just enough so that it does not move around. Have the children wear smocks.

Give each child a piece of chalk and let him *"draw"* for as long as he wants. When he has finished, have him *"erase"* his drawing with an eraser. If he wants to draw again, give him a piece of chalk and he's all ready.

VARIATION

MORE ERASING

Instead of using erasers, let the children use slightly damp sponges. Be careful not to let the box get too wet.

SIDEWALK CHALK RECIPE

mix ~ form

SUPPLIES AND MATERIALS

Styrofoam cups
Sturdy mixing spoon or paint stir stick
Plaster of Paris
Different colors of dry tempera paint
Water
Molds, such as:
    Small dixie cups
    Plastic popsicle molds
    Small plastic cups from
        lemonade mixes,
        puddings, and yogurt

MAKE SIDEWALK CHALK

1. Fill the styrofoam cup about 3/4 full of plaster.

2. Add about one tablespoon of dry tempera paint to the plaster.

3. Mix the dry paint and plaster together until thoroughly blended.

4. Slowly add water, stirring the whole time, until the mixture is that of cake batter.

5. Pour the mixture into the mold/s. Let the mold set for two hours or until the mixture hardens. Pop out your new chalk!

6. Repeat the process for more chalk. Change colors by mixing different dry tempera with the plaster.

STORE SIDEWALK CHALK

Keep the chalk in a resealable bag.
Keep it handy to take outside for
quick and easy art activities.

CHALK ON SIDEWALKS

SIZE OF GROUP: Any size group.
DO THE ACTIVITY: Outside

SUPPLIES AND MATERIALS

Sidewalk chalk (See recipe page 176)
Plastic milk bottles for half to all of the children
House paint brushes for half to all of the children
Water

PREPARATION

☛ Cut the milk bottles into water buckets. (See illustration.)

ACTIVITY

When the children want to *"draw"* on the sidewalk give them chalk and let them draw. After each child has finished, have him give you his piece of chalk. Help him fill a bucket with water. Give him the water and a paint brush, and let him *"wash-off"* his chalk drawing.

CHALK DOTS

draw
~
scribble
~
dot

SIZE OF GROUP: Any size group.
DO THE ACTIVITY: Outside

SUPPLIES AND MATERIALS

Sidewalk chalk (See recipe on page 176)

PREPARATION

None

ACTIVITY

When the children want to draw, give them a piece of chalk to *"draw and scribble"* with. After several children have gathered, you take a piece of chalk and begin chanting *"dot, dot, dot, dot..."* as you make dots on the sidewalk. The children who want to, will join you and start to make their dots as they chant *"dot, dot, dot...."*

VARIATION

MORE CHALKING

Instead of chanting *"dot, dot, dot...,"* chant:

- ☛ *"Scribble, scribble, scribble..."*
- ☛ *"Line, line, line..."*
- ☛ *"Hard, hard, hard..."*
- ☛ *"Soft, soft, soft..."*
- ☛ *"Back and forth, back and forth, back and forth..."*

CHALK CARS

SIZE OF GROUP: Individual or small group
DO THE ACTIVITY: Outside

SUPPLIES AND MATERIALS

Sidewalk chalk (See recipe on page 176)
Large toy cars
Masking tape

PREPARATION

☛ Make the Chalk Cars

1. Stand a piece of chalk in the front or back of a car.

2. Wind a piece of tape around the car several times, so the chalk is firmly attached.

3. Repeat the process for each car.

4. Park the CHALK CARS in a wagon.

ACTIVITY

Use chalk to mark off a large track on your playground. Have the wagon of cars nearby. Give the children CHALK CARS and let each of them *"drive"* his car back and forth and around the track, *"marking"* the track as he goes.

VARIATION
MORE CHALK CARS

Instead of taping one piece of sidewalk chalk to the back or front of each vehicle, tape:

☛ 2 or 3 pieces to the back or front of each one.
☛ The same color chalk to the back and front of each vehicle.

CHALK TRACING AND ERASING

SIZE OF GROUP: Individual children
DO THE ACTIVITY: Outside

SUPPLIES AND MATERIALS

Sidewalk chalk (See page 176.)
Plastic milk bottles
Scrub brushes

PREPARATION

☛ Cut the milk bottles into water buckets. (See illustration.)

ACTIVITY

Have a child lie down on the sidewalk. Using sidewalk chalk, *"trace"* her body. As you are tracing, periodically stop and ask the child, *"What body part am I tracing now?"* Let the child answer and then continue tracing. Keep tracing and stopping until you have traced her whole body on the sidewalk. Help her get up. Talk with her about her tracing. Let her color herself with different colors of sidewalk chalk.   When she is finished, let her give herself a bath. Fill a milk bottle bucket about half full of water. Let her use the water and a scrub brush to *"wash"* herself clean.

HINT: The tracing and washing are both fun and valuable. Children love to do both activities.

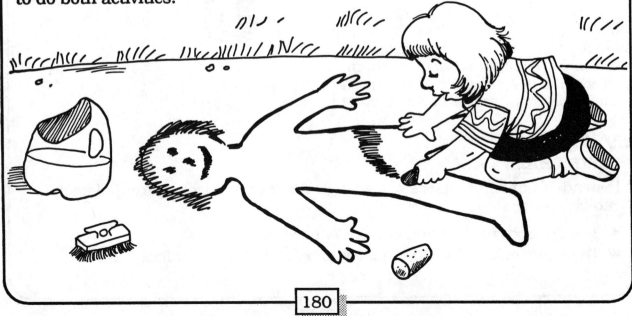

CHALK ON BRICKS

smudge
~
erase

SIZE OF GROUP: Individuals or small group
DO THE ACTIVITY: Outside

SUPPLIES AND MATERIALS

Sidewalk chalk (See recipe on page 176.)
Bricks
Plastic milk bottles
Old dish brushes

PREPARATION

☛ Cut the milk bottles into water buckets. (See illustration.)

ACTIVITY

Put the bricks in a shady area of the playground. Fill each milk bottle bucket with a little water. Put a dish brush in each one. Let the children *"smudge"* chalk all over the bricks and then *"wash"* them with water and dish brushes. If a child wants to smudge again, give him another piece of chalk.

SAFETY HINT: Remind the children not to pick up the bricks, stones, etc.

VARIATION

MORE CHALKING
Instead of smudging on bricks, use:

- ☛ Cement blocks
- ☛ Giant stones
- ☛ Garden paving or stepping stones
- ☛ Flagstones
- ☛ Brick wall

Using Easels

EASEL PAINT RECIPE

mix ~ store

SUPPLIES AND MATERIALS

1-lb container of powdered tempera paint
1/4 to 1/2 cup of liquid starch
1/4 to 1/2 cup water
1 or 2T of soap powder
Blender or large pitcher and egg beater

MAKE EASEL PAINT

1. Pour the powdered paint in the blender/pitcher.

2. Pour in the liquid starch and "mix" the two ingredients.

3. Add half the water and blend again. Add more water and blend to get the consistency you want.

4. Lastly pour in the powdered soap and blend. (This helps to thicken the paint a little, but more importantly helps make washing easier.)

5. Repeat the process for each color.

STORE THE PAINT

Pour each color of tempera paint into a plastic milk bottle and cap it. Keep all of the paint on a shelf away from the children, but near the art area. Pour the paint into small easel containers as you need it.

HINT: Use this tempera paint recipe for easel painting and other painting activities.

184

VEGETABLE DYE PAINT RECIPE

mix ~ store

SUPPLIES AND MATERIALS

1t powdered vegetable food dye
    (school supply store or catalogue)
4T water
Liquid starch
Powdered soap
Large pitcher

MAKE THE PAINT

1. Spoon the food dye into
   the pitcher.

2. Add the water and *"mix"*
   until the food dye is dissolved.

3. Slowly pour and stir as much
   liquid starch into the mixture needed to
   reach the paint consistency you are looking for.

4. Stir a little powdered soap into the paint. (Easier to wash out paint
   stains.)

5. Repeat the process for each color.

HINTS:

☛ You can blend the different vegetable dyes together to create different
  colors of paint:
      Yellow and a little red makes orange.
      Red and a little blue makes purple.
      Green and a little red makes brown.
☛ You can substitute food coloring for the vegetable dye, however the paint
  colors are not as brilliant.

STORE THE PAINT

Pour each color of vegetable dye paint into a plastic milk bottle and cap it.
Keep all of the milk bottles on a shelf away from the children, but near the
art area. Pour the paint into small easel containers as you need it.

TEXTURED EASEL PAINT RECIPE

SUPPLIES AND MATERIALS

Pitcher
Easel paint
White glue
Different, finely granulated textures, such as:

Fine sand	Sawdust
Cornstarch	Soap powder
Coffee ground	Tea leaves

MAKE THE TEXTURED PAINT

1. Pour the paint into a pitcher.

2. *"Mix-in"* one texture. Add more if the paint is too smooth.

3. Squeeze in a little white glue and stir it into the textured paint. (This will help the texture adhere to the paper.)

4. Repeat the process with every color.

HINTS:

☛ The soap powder makes a very rich, thick paint, and gives you a tiny dotted effect.

☛ The coffee grounds and tea leaves make a great texture with white paint. The black texture is very striking.

☛ The cornstarch makes a thick paint that is a little dull.

☛ You'll probably need to add water to the paint when you mix it with sawdust, or the paint will be too thick for easel paint.

STORE THE TEXTURED PAINT

Pour the textured paint into the easel containers and cover them immediately. Let the children use them within the next several days.

SCENTED EASEL PAINT RECIPE

mix ~ store

SUPPLIES AND MATERIALS

Pitcher
Easel paint
Different scents, such as:
    Extracts
        Vanilla
        Peppermint
        Spearmint
        Wintergreen
    Spices
        Cinnamon
        Clove
        Pumpkin
    Lemon juice
    Unsweetened, powdered
        drink mixes
    Unsweetened gelatins
    Baby powder/talcum powder

MAKE SCENTED EASEL PAINT

(Make this paint just before the children arrive. This will insure that the scent is still strong, plus it will be fun and inviting for the children to smell it as they arrive.)

1. Pour the paint into a pitcher.

2. Sprinkle in one dry or liquid scent.

3. *"Mix"* the scent and paint. If the smell is not strong enough, stir in more scent, a little at a time.

4. Repeat the process for each paint you want to scent.

STORE THE SCENTED PAINT

Pour the scented paint into the easel containers and cover them immediately. Let the children use them the day you mixed in the scent.

STAND AT
THE EASEL

SIZE OF GROUP: Individual children
DO THE ACTIVITY: At the Easel

SUPPLIES AND MATERIALS

Easel paint
Short-handled brushes
Easel paper

PREPARATION

☛ Pour several colors of paint into easel containers. Have a stubby brush for each container.

ACTIVITY

Put one paint container/brush in each easel tray. Set the other paint containers on a high shelf. Have the children put on their smocks.

Let the children *"brush and dot"* the paper for as long as they want. After each child has painted for awhile, ask her if she would like to paint with a different color. If she says, *"Yes,"* have her hand you the container of paint she is using, and you hand her another color. Now she's ready to continue painting.

SIT AT THE TABLE EASEL

brush
~
dot

SIZE OF GROUP: Individual children
DO THE ACTIVITY: At the Art Table

SUPPLIES AND MATERIALS

Easel paint
Short-handled brushes
Easel paper

PREPARATION

☛ Pour several colors of paint into easel containers. Have a stubby brush for each container.

☛ If you do not have a commercially-built easel, make one for your classroom.

MAKE THE EASEL:

Stand two sides so that they form a right angle, with one side on the table and the other one sticking up straight. Slant the third side over to touch the side which is standing up. Fold the top of the straight side over the slanted side. Tape the fold to the slanted side.

ACTIVITY

Spread and tape newspaper to the table. Set the easels on the paper and tape it down. Have one container of paint and a brush on each side of each easel. Have the children put on their smocks. Let the children *"brush and dot"* for as long as each would like.

PAINTING OUTSIDE AT THE EASEL

brush ~ dot

SIZE OF GROUP: Individual
DO THE ACTIVITY: At the Easel

SUPPLIES AND MATERIALS

Easel paint
Stubby brushes
Easel paper
Different types of easels, such as:
    Table easel
    Floor easel
    Fence
    Side of building

PREPARATION

☛ Decide what easel activities
you want to do outside and gather the
supplies and materials. For example:

1. If you want the children to paint the side of a building or the fence, cut a long piece of butcher paper and roll it up.

2. If you want the children to paint at one of the easels, simply roll up the easel paper.

ACTIVITY

Carry the easels (if necessary), paper, paint, smocks, and brushes outside. Set them up:

1. Tape the butcher paper to the building.

2. Clothespin the butcher paper to fence.

3. Tape the table easel to an outside table.

4. Place the floor easel where you want it.

When a child wants to paint, have him put on a smock. Hand him a container of paint and a brush, and let him *"brush and dot"* the paper for as long as he would like. Ask him if he'd like to paint with a different color. If he does, switch containers with him and let him continue.

MORE THAN EASEL PAPER

brush ~ dot

SIZE OF GROUP: Individual children
DO THE ACTIVITY: At the Easel

SUPPLIES AND MATERIALS

Easel paint
Short-handled brushes
Different easel paper, such as:
- Paper grocery bags
- Miscellaneous pieces of large cardboard
- Wrapping paper
- Wallpaper
- Old file folders
- Black/white newspaper pages

PREPARATION

☛ Cut the paper to fit on your easel/s.
☛ Pour different colors of paint in easel containers.

ACTIVITY

Put one paint container/brush in each easel tray. Set the other paint containers on a high shelf. Have the paper you are using that day quickly available. Remind the children to put on their smocks.

Help each child clip his easel paper to the easel. Let him feel the paper. Tell him what type of paper he will be painting on. Ask him if he knows where you might have gotten the paper. Has he ever seen that type of paper before?

Let the children *"brush and dot"* the paint on this special paper for as long as each would like. After each child has painted for awhile, ask him if he would like to paint with a different color. If he says, *"Yes,"* exchange paints with him and let him continue; if *"No"* let him continue with the color he has.

HOLES AT THE EASEL

SIZE OF GROUP: Individual children
DO THE ACTIVITY: At the Easel

SUPPLIES AND MATERIALS

Easel paint
Short-handled brushes
Easel paper

PREPARATION

☛ Cut the Holes In the Easel Paper
  1. Loosely fold a piece of paper in half.
  2. Cut a hole somewhere along the fold.
  3. Unfold the paper and lay it flat.
  4. Repeat the process for each piece of paper.

ACTIVITY

Put the *"holey"* paper near the easel. Set one container of paint with one brush in each easel tray. Have the children put on their smocks.

When a child comes to the easel, tell him you have "holey" paper for him to paint on today. First clip an un-cut piece of easel paper to the easel. Then clip the *"holey"* paper on top of the solid one.

Let the child *"brush and dot"* the *"holey"* paper for as long as he would like.

HINTS: Some children will paint the paper under the hole, and others will paint the paper with the hole cut in it.

VARIATION

MORE "HOLEY" PAINTING
☛ The first several times you do this activity, cut all the holes in the paper the same size and shape. From then on cut different holes:

☛ Cut one large hole in each paper
☛ Cut holes in different places in the paper.
☛ Cut several smaller holes
☛ Cut different-shaped holes

192

SHAPES AT THE EASEL

brush ~ dot

SIZE OF GROUP: Individual children
DO THE ACTIVITY: At the Easel

SUPPLIES AND MATERIALS

Easel paint
Stubby brushes
Easel paper

PREPARATION

☞ Cut the Shapes Out of
Easel Paper

1. Pick a shape, such as a circle.

2. Cut all the easel paper for
   the activity the same size
   and shape, such as
   giant circles.

ACTIVITY

Put the shape paper near
the easel. Have the
children put on smocks.

When a child comes to paint, help
her clip the paper to the easel. Tell
her that you cut the paper into a special
shape --name the shape, such as "*a really
big circle.*" Let her "*brush and dot*" the circle for as long
as she would like. As she's painting you might comment about:

☞ Where she is painting. "*You are painting in the middle of the circle.*"

☞ How she is painting. "*You are moving your brush around and around in
circles, just like the shape of your paper.*"

193

CRAYONS AT THE EASEL

scribble

SIZE OF GROUP: Individual children
DO THE ACTIVITY: At the easel

SUPPLIES AND MATERIALS

Jumbo crayons
Easel paper
Yarn

PREPARATION

☛ String Each Crayon

1. Use a plastic knife and cut a notch around the top of the crayon.

2. Tie a 2-3 foot piece of yarn in the notch.

3. Repeat the process for the other crayons.

ACTIVITY

Tie one or two crayons to the top of the easel, so they hang down to the bottom. Clip the paper to the easel.

Let the children use the crayons and *"scribble"* over the entire sheet for as long as each would like.

After each child has finished, ask her where she would like you to write her name. Write it where she indicates.

194

BUBBLES AT THE EASEL

dip ~ blow

SIZE OF GROUP: Individual children
DO THE ACTIVITY: At the Easel

SUPPLIES AND MATERIALS

Commercial bubble blowing solution
At least one small, unbreakable
 bottle with a lid for each child
Food coloring
Paper towels
Lots of bubble wands
 (several for each child)
Easel paper

PREPARATION

☛ Prepare the Bubble Solution

1. Divide the solution into small
 bottles so each is about 1/3 full.

2. Add 1/8t of food coloring
 to each bottle.

3. Cover the bottle and shake the
 solution until it is colored

ACTIVITY

Put the bottles of bubble solution on a shelf near the easel.
Have the children put on their smocks.

When each child wants to BLOW BUBBLES, help him clip his paper to the
easel and hand him a bottle of bubbles. Show him how to slowly pull out
the wand, gently blow, and then dip it back into the bottle to get more
solution. Let him do it several times while you are near him.

Let him continue to *"dip and blow"* for as long as he would like, making
colored marks all over his paper.

HINT: Because children are just learning to blow, they often put their
mouths on the wands. To prevent the spread of germs, let each child use a
different bottle of solution and wand each time he BUBBLE BLOWS.

WHITE "PAINT" AT THE EASEL

SIZE OF GROUP: Individual children
DO THE ACTIVITY: At the Easel

SUPPLIES AND MATERIALS

Dark easel paper, such as dark
   butcher or shelf paper
White shoe polish in bottles with
   sponge applicators
Liquid detergent

PREPARATION

☛ Cut the dark paper into
   appropriate sizes for your easel.

☛ Pour a little liquid detergent into
   the bottles of shoe polish, and then
   give them several shakes.

ACTIVITY

Put the shoe polish bottles and dark paper on a shelf near the easel.

When a child wants to paint, have her put on a smock, and then help her
clip paper to the easel. Hand her a bottle of shoe polish. Show her how to
pull out the applicator and then put it back in the bottle. Let her do it
several times.

Now let her *"smear and dot"* the dark paper with white polish for as long as
she would like.

HINTS:

☛ The white shoe polish on dark paper is very striking. Children often like
   to do this for a long time.

☛ If the shoe polish is too runny, mix-in a little white glue.

☛ If you run out of white shoe polish, fill the shoe bottles with
   thinned-down white tempera paint.

PAINTING AT THE FENCE EASEL

SIZE OF GROUP: Small group
DO THE ACTIVITY: Outside

SUPPLIES AND MATERIALS

Corrugated cardboard
Tempera paint
Easel brushes
Large pieces of paper
Clip clothespins

PREPARATION

☞ Cut several very large
  sheets of corrugated
  cardboard to use as
  "easels" on your fence.

☞ Pour tempera paint into
  juice cans, and put them
  in a cardboard soda
  pop carrier.

ACTIVITY

Clip the corrugated board low on the fence. Set the paint and brushes by the board. Have the children put on smocks before they paint.

When a child wants to paint, help her clip a piece of paper to the cardboard, and then let her *"paint"* for as long as she wants. After she's finished, help her hang her painting on the fence to dry.

VARIATION

Instead of painting, let the children crayon or chalk at the fence.

Appendices

Art Charts

Permanent Supplies

Balls
Beach towels
Berry baskets
Bingo blotters
Bubble pack
Bubble wands
Bus tubs
Canvas drop cloths
Castors
Chalkboards - all sizes
Clothesline
Clothespins
Cookie cutters
Cookie sheets
Corks - all sizes
Deodorant bottles
Dish tubs
Door mats
Erasers
Fly swatters
Forks
Formica
Full length mirror
Golf balls
Jar lids
Kitchen utensils
Ice cube trays
Ink pads/stamps
Marbles
Measuring cups
Metal hangers
Mittens
Mixing bowls
Muffin tins

Oil cloth
Pails
Paint brushes - all sizes
Paint rollers - all sizes
Panelling
Pegboard
Pie pans
Pitchers
Plastic carpet protector
Plastic place mats
Plastic trays
Popsicle molds
Potato mashers
Pump-type bottles
Record player
Rubber bath mats
Salt shakers
Scissors
Scoops
Scrub brushes
Shaker bottles with
    different size holes
Sheet cake pan
Spatulas
Spoons - all sizes
Sponges
Sponge brushes
Spray bottles
Squeeze bottles - all sizes
Stools
Toaster
Toy vehicles
Warming tray
Whisks

Building Blocks
Elgin, Illinois 60123

Disposable Supplies

All types of paper
Appliance boxes
Baby powder
Bed sheets
Box tops
Bricks
Bubble pack
Bubble blowing solution
Cardboard
Chalk
Comic paper
Confetti
Corrugated boxes
Cotton batting/swabs
Crayons
Dish soap
Dowel rods
Egg cartons
Fabrics - all types
Food coloring
Large pieces of styrofoam
Large trash bags
Lipstick
Liquid starch
Magazines
Masking tape
Paint

Paper plates
Paper towels
Paper tubes
Paste
Pencils
Petroleum jelly
Plastic milk bottles
Polyester batting
Popsicle sticks
Ribbon
Rubber bands
Shallow boxes
Shaving cream
Shaving gel
Shoe boxes
Soap powder
Sponges - all sizes
Spools
String
Styrofoam peanuts
Styrofoam trays
Tablecloths
Tongue depressors
Twine
White glue
Yarn

Building Blocks

Elgin, Illinois 60123

Paper

Adding machine tape
Adhesive paper
All types of scrap paper
Aluminum foil
Box tops
Butcher paper
Cardboard
Cardboard trays
Cardboard tubes-all sizes
Coffee filters
Construction paper
Corrugated boxes
Corrugated cardboard
Desk blotters
Duplicating paper
Easel paper
Egg cartons
File folders
Fingerpaint paper
Foil wallpaper
Greeting cards

Grocery bags
Mailing paper
Manilla paper
Newspaper
Newsprint
Paper bags
Paper plates-large/small
Paper towels
Pizza boards
Placemats
Sandpaper
Shallow boxes
Shelf paper
Studio photographer's
   background paper
Tagboard
Table cloths
Tissue paper
Wallpaper
Waxed paper
Wrapping paper
   (heavy-duty)

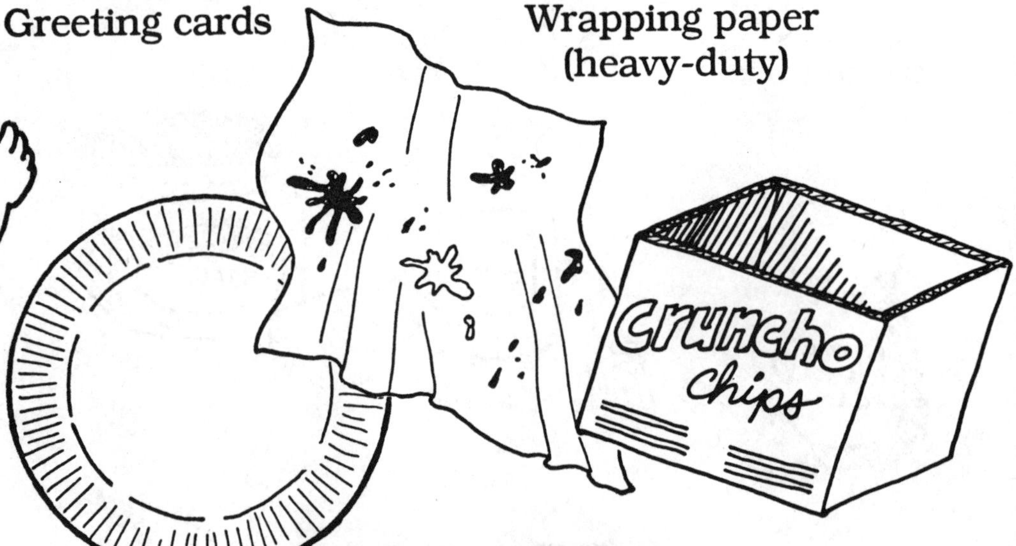

BUILDING BLOCKS

Elgin, Illinois   60123

Collage Materials

All types of paper
  (See paper list)
Bark
Bottle caps
Cardboard tubes
Confetti
Corduroy
Corks
Craft feathers
Cupcake liners
Denim
Egg cartons
Fabric - all types
Felt
Foam pieces
Greeting cards
Heavy yarn
Jar lids
Large buttons
Large paper clips

Leather
Leaves
Popsicle sticks
Ribbons
Rope
Rubber bands
Sandpaper
Small boxes (raisins,
  candy, etc.)
Spools
Sticks
Straws
Streamers
String
Styrofoam peanuts
Styrofoam trays
Tongue depressors
Twine
Wood pieces (smooth)
Yarn

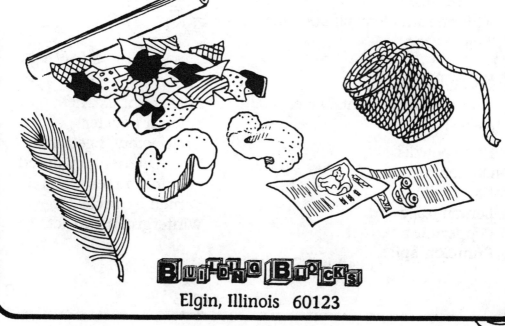

Building Blocks

Elgin, Illinois 60123

Textures, Scents, And Containers

CONTAINERS

Baby wipe boxes
Brownie pans
Bus tubs
Coffee cans
Dish tubs
Glue squeeze bottles
Ketchup/mustard
    squeeze bottles
Margarine tubs
Messy trays
Mixing bowls
Pie pans
Pitchers
Plastic milk bottles
Soft perm bottles
Sturdy boxes - all sizes
Styrofoam meat/produce trays
Tuna cans
Unbreakable shaker jars -
    all width holes
Wide-mouth clear plastic jars
Yogurt tubs

SCENTS

(Add to doughs, paints, glues, and pastes)

Baby powder
Cinnamon spice
Clove spice
Lemon juice
Peppermint extract
Pumpkin spice

TEXTURES

(Add to doughs, pastes, and paints)

Aquarium gravel
Bird seed
Confetti circles
Crushed egg shells
Dried coffee grounds
Dried evergreen needles
Dried field corn
Dried tea grounds
Grass seed
Pebbles
Powdered soap
Sand
Sawdust
Sequins
Soap powder
Talcum powder

Spearmint extract
Talcum powder
Unsweetened gelatins
Unsweetened powdered
    drink mixes
Vanilla extract
Wintergreen extract

BUILDING BLOCKS

Elgin, Illinois   60123

Paint With:

UTENSILS

Bingo blotters
Chair/table castors
Combs
Corn cobs
Daubers
Deodorant bottles
Dowel rods - all sizes
Feather dusters - small
Fly swatters
Golf balls
Hair rollers
Ice cubes
Jar lids
Kitchen utensils
Marbles
Paint rollers - all sizes
Pine branches
Ping pong balls
Rolling pins
Rubber balls
Scouring pads
Sponges
Strings
Tennis balls
Toy vehicles
Twine

BRUSHES

Back brushes
Bottle brushes
Dish brushes
Dog and cat brushes
Eye lash brushes
Eye liner brushes
House painting brushes
Lipstick brushes
Mustache brushes
Paint brushes - all widths
Scrub brushes
Shaving cream brushes
Shoe polish brushes
Shoe shine brushes
Snow scrapper brushes
Sponge brushes
Stubby handle paint brushes
Toilet bowl brushes
Toenail and fingernail brushes
Toothbrushes
Vacuum cleaner brushes

PRINTING PROPS

Berry baskets
Bingo blotters
Cookie cutters
Film canisters
Funnels
Kitchen utensils

Pumpkin rhine pieces
  (add fork handle)
Puzzle pieces with handles
Sponges (thick or add a handle)
Spools
Wide jar lids

BUILDING BLOCKS
Elgin, Illinois 60123

Library

The Circle Time Series

by Liz and Dick Wilmes. Hundreds of activities for large and small groups of children. Each book is filled with Language and Active games, Fingerplays, Songs, Stories, Snacks, and more. A great resource for every library shelf.

Circle Time Book

Captures the spirit of 39 holidays and seasons.
ISBN 0-943452-00-7   **$ 12.95**

Everyday Circle Times

Over 900 ideas. Choose from 48 topics divided into 7 sections: self-concept, basic concepts, animals, foods, science, occupations, and recreation.
ISBN 0-943452-01-5   **$16.95**

More Everyday Circle Times

Divided into the same 7 sections as EVERYDAY. Features new topics such as Birds and Pizza, plus all new ideas for some familiar topics contained in EVERYDAY.
ISBN 0-943452-14-7   **$16.95**

Yearful of Circle Times

52 different topics to use weekly, by seasons, or mixed throughout the year. New Friends, Signs of Fall, Snowfolk Fun, and much more.
ISBN 0-943452-10-4   **$16.95**

Paint Without Brushes

by Liz and Dick Wilmes. Use common materials which you already have. Discover the painting possibilities in your classroom! PAINT WITHOUT BRUSHES gives your children open-ended art activities to explore paint in lots of creative ways. A valuable art resource. One you'll want to use daily.
ISBN 0-943452-15-5   **$12.95**

Gifts, Cards, and Wraps

by Wilmes and Zavodsky. Help the children sparkle with the excitement of gift giving. Filled with thoughtful gifts, unique wraps, and special cards which the children can make and give. They're sure to bring smiles.
ISBN 0-943452-06-6   **$ 7.95**

Everyday Bulletin Boards

by Wilmes and Moehling. Features borders, murals, backgrounds, and other open-ended art to display on your bulletin boards. Plus board ideas with patterns, which teachers can make and use to enhance their curriculum.
ISBN 0-943452-09-0   **$ 12.95**

Exploring Art

by Liz and Dick Wilmes. EXPLORING ART is divided by months. Over 250 art ideas for paint, chalk, doughs, scissors, and more. Easy to set-up in your classroom.
ISBN 0-943452-05-8   **$19.95**

C I R C L E   T I M E

A R T

2's Experience Series

by Liz and Dick Wilmes. An exciting series developed especially for toddlers and two's.

2's Experience Art

Art for toddlers and two's! Over 150 activities... Scribble, Paint, Smear, Mix, Tear, Mold, Paste, and more. Plus lots of recipes and hints.
ISBN 0-943452-21-X   **$ 16.95**

2's Experience Dramatic Play

Dress up and pretend! Let toddlers and two's play hundreds of imaginary characters... firefighters, campers, bus drivers, and more.
ISBN 0-943452-20-1   **$12.95**

2's Experience Felt Board Fun

Hundreds of extra large patterns accompany special stories, rhymes, and activities... teddy bears, birthdays, farm animals, and more.
ISBN 0-943452-19-8   **$14.95**

2's Experience Fingerplays

Wonderful collection of easy fingerplays with accompanying games and large FINGERPLAY CARDS— illustrations for one side and words/movement for the other..
ISBN 0-943452-18-X   **$12.95**

Learning Centers

by Liz and Dick Wilmes. Hundreds of open-ended activities to quickly involve and excite your children. You'll use it every time you plan and whenever you need a quick, additional activity. A must for every teacher's bookshelf.
ISBN 0-943452-13-9   **$19.95**

Felt Board Fun

by Liz and Dick Wilmes. Make your felt board come alive. Discover how versatile it is as the children become involved with a wide range of activities. This unique book has over 150 ideas with accompanying patterns.
ISBN 0-943452-02-3   **$16.95**

Table & Floor Games

by Liz and Dick Wilmes. 32 easy-to-make, fun-to-play table/floor games with accompanying patterns ready to trace or photocopy. Teach beginning concepts such as matching, counting, colors, alphabet recognition, sorting and so on.
ISBN 0-943452-16-3   **$19.95**

Activities Unlimited

by Adler, Caton, and Cleveland. Create an enthusiasm for learning! Hundreds of innovative activities to help your children develop fine and gross motor skills, increase their language, become self-reliant, and play cooperatively. Whether you're a beginning teacher or a veteran, this book will quickly become one of your favorites.
ISBN 0-943452-17-1   **$16.95**

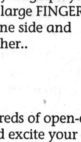